Drowning in Drama

Drowning in Drama

Jonah and the Drama Triangle

Jim Cooper Jr.

Foreword by Ingrid Faro

WIPF & STOCK · Eugene, Oregon

DROWNING IN DRAMA
Jonah and the Drama Triangle

Copyright © 2025 Jim Cooper Jr. All rights reserved. Except for brief quotations in critical publications or reviews, no part of this book may be reproduced in any manner without prior written permission from the publisher. Write: Permissions, Wipf and Stock Publishers, 199 W. 8th Ave., Suite 3, Eugene, OR 97401.

Wipf & Stock
An Imprint of Wipf and Stock Publishers
199 W. 8th Ave., Suite 3
Eugene, OR 97401

www.wipfandstock.com

PAPERBACK ISBN: 979-8-3852-4434-8
HARDCOVER ISBN: 979-8-3852-4435-5
EBOOK ISBN: 979-8-3852-4436-2

VERSION NUMBER 08/08/25

All Scripture quotations, unless otherwise indicated, are taken from the Holy Bible, New International Version®, NIV®. Copyright © 1973, 1978, 1984, 2011 by Biblica, Inc.™ Used by permission of Zondervan. All rights reserved worldwide. www.zondervan.com. The "NIV" and "New International Version" are trademarks registered in the United States Patent and Trademark Office by Biblica, Inc.™

Scripture quotations marked (ESV) are from the ESV® Bible (The Holy Bible, English Standard Version®), © 2001 by Crossway, a publishing ministry of Good News Publishers. ESV Text Edition: 2025. The ESV text may not be quoted in any publication made available to the public by a Creative Commons license. The ESV may not be translated in whole or in part into any other language. Used by permission. All rights reserved.

Scripture quotations marked (MSG) are taken from *The Message*, copyright © 1993, 2002, 2018 by Eugene H. Peterson. Used by permission of NavPress. All rights reserved. Represented by Tyndale House Publishers.

Scripture quotations marked (NCV) are taken from the New Century Version®. Copyright © 2005 by Thomas Nelson. Used by permission. All rights reserved.

Contents

Foreword by Ingrid Faro | vii
Acknowledgments | xi
Introduction | xiii

Part 1: Jonah: The Victim

1   On the Run: Jonah's Flight from God | 3
2   Repurposed Pain: How God Uses Pain as a Tool for Transformation and Growth | 11
3   Passing Peace: The Deceptive, Parasitic Nature of False Peace and Its Detrimental Damage | 16
4   The Transformative Power of Vulnerability: Surrendering Our Fear and Hurt | 21
5   True Peace: The Peace That Abides When in Harmony with God, Self, and Community | 28
6   Enduring the Process: Salvation, Restoration, and Surrender | 36

Part 2: Sailors: The Rescuers

7   Fear-Driven Responsibility: How Fear and Misplaced Guilt Drive Us to Take On Others' Responsibilities | 45
8   The Enabling Trap: Even Well-Intentioned Rescuing May Hinder True Healing | 53

9 Good Intentions vs. God's Intent:
   The Limits of Human Intention | 58
10 Surrendering Control: The Freedom and Peace of Trusting
   God's Greater Plan over Our Own Desired Outcomes | 64
11 Misplaced Sympathy: How Misplaced
   Sympathies Hinder God's Work | 71

Part 3: Ninevites: The Persecutors

12 Blinded by Greatness: The Allure of Greatness
   Obscures Moral Clarity | 79
13 The Persecutor's Privilege: The Responsibility
   of People in Power | 89
14 A Propensity for Propaganda: How Power Drives
   the Creation of False Images to Coerce and Control | 95
15 Violent Coercion: Examining the Persecutor's Spectrum
   of Violence and Urging Self-Reflection | 99
16 Submission of Power: How Surrendering
   to God's Vision Transforms Personal Power
   into a Source of True Strength | 104

Part 4: Christ and the Winner's Triangle

17 Our Vulnerable Creator: Revealing Jesus
   as the One Who Breaks the Cycle of Drama | 115

Bibliography | 121

Foreword

I MET JIM COOPER when he came on campus as a doctoral student at Northern Seminary, where I teach Old Testament. When Jim told me about his work on trauma in the book of Jonah, I was a bit skeptical but curious. For many, the Bible can feel dry or removed from significance to our daily challenges and struggles. Reading the Bible, especially by scholars and "professional" Christians, is often approached without seeking to apply its perspectives and narratives to the stories of our personal lives. But this is not the path Jim took! *Drowning in Drama* is a unique and highly relatable reading of Jonah and its key characters that assists the reader in seeing themselves and those involved in a cycle of trauma in a way that enlightens, instructs, and engenders a positive path for change.

One of my specialized areas of research and ministry is the problem of evil in the Bible. Within that is trauma and abuse. For the eleven years that I taught biblical Hebrew, the book of Jonah was often my chosen text for advanced Hebrew exegesis and study. I understood why Jonah ran from God's assignment to prophesy to the people of Nineveh, the capital of the Assyrian Empire. The Assyrians were known for the gruesome treatment of their enemies, including women and children. They aimed to terrify and shock people into submission through their brutality.

When people criticize Jonah, I describe his situation as someone whose family had been tortured and killed by ISIS being told by God to go to those very terrorists with a message of forgiveness

Foreword

and salvation. This would not be easy! Especially since the Assyrians had been brutalizing the entire nation of Israel for decades.

The traumas Jonah saw and experienced had to be massive, continuous, and complex. Jonah knew God was compassionate and merciful, and he was not prepared to be God's agent in extending forgiveness to them for their vile acts. We can have compassion on Jonah's unwillingness to show them mercy.

But this is just the starting place for Jim Cooper's insights in *Drowning in Drama*. Even though I was aware of the terror tactics of Assyrian warfare, I had not thought of looking at the entire book of Jonah through the lens of trauma studies. These insights were born out of his and his wife's own experiences with trauma and betrayal.

Jim shares his personal stories, including the deep betrayal his wife experienced within their institution—an institution in which both he and his wife continue to serve. As they worked through the emotional and spiritual fallout, Jim found a powerful resonance between the biblical story of Jonah and two frameworks that helped them make sense of their experience: Stephen Karpman's "Drama Triangle," which maps the destructive dynamics of relational conflict, and Acey Choy's "Winner's Triangle," which offers a path toward healthier, more redemptive relationships. Jim provides a unique and deeply thoughtful reflection of Jonah through these tools. Thankfully, in their hardship, he and his wife formed a unified team to steer their way through the pain and navigate their hurts.

The result, *Drowning in Drama*, is an invitation and a guide for self-reflection written in a way that drew me in, brought to light many situations and people, and illuminated my own role when participating in relational drama. Each drama triangle offers opportunities to turn bent relationships toward healthy ones. Observing the characters in Jonah through the lens of the Drama and Winner's Triangles, as illustrated through Jim's stories in this book, opens the aperture to see our own lives with greater clarity.

As I read through this book, images of events and relationships in my own life came to mind, facilitating my ability to see

Foreword

how I and others at times have stepped into each role in the Drama Triangle, alternately as Victim, Rescuer, and Persecutor. Conversations with friends suffering from and causing hurtful interactions also came to mind and played out alongside the stories and words of Jonah, the seafaring men, and the Ninevites. In each scene, I saw God's outstretched hand inviting all to slow down, listen, and shift, as Jim reflects on his own life while reading Jonah in light of the two triangles.

Ingrid Faro, PhD, MDiv
Professor of Old Testament, Northern Seminary, Lisle, Illinois
June 2025

Acknowledgments

To my wife, Heidi—
Your courage has been a revelation. In the face of betrayal, you chose vulnerability over silence and truth over bitterness. You created space for healing—not only for yourself but also for many others. Through your life, I came to see Jesus more clearly: not as one who avoids pain, but as one who enters it with redemptive love. This book exists because of your faithfulness. Thank you for your strength, your surrender, and your unwavering trust in God.

To Dr. Ingrid Faro—
Thank you for believing in me and giving this work a place to grow. Your careful review, wise edits, and steady support made this project possible.

To A. R. Williams—
Thank you for helping get this project off the ground, and even more so, for believing in me from the beginning when I first shared my desire to write. Your encouragement helped set this in motion.

To A. J. Swoboda, Sam Black, and David Fitch—
Your support and encouragement mean more than I can express. Thank you for lending your voices and affirming the message of this work.

Acknowledgments

To Dara Powers Parker—
Your editorial insight and attention to detail helped bring clarity and life to these pages. Thank you for the time and care you invested in shaping this manuscript.

Introduction

"My son, give me your heart, and let your eyes observe my ways."
—Proverbs 23:26 (ESV)

"At fifteen life had taught me undeniably that surrender, in its place, was as honorable as resistance, especially if one had no choice."
—Maya Angelou, *I Know Why the Caged Bird Sings*

FIVE YEARS AGO, MY wife and I—ordained pastors with more than twenty-five years of experience in ministry—found ourselves caught in something that felt far bigger than us. It was like being pulled into a storm we didn't see coming, disoriented by waves of betrayal, silence, and grief. At times, we felt overwhelmed—like we were drowning in something we couldn't name.

The experience cracked something open in me. My vulnerability came bubbling to the surface, ripping through the masks I typically wore to conceal it. While still awkwardly clinging to my part to play in the story, I was introduced to the Drama Triangle, a social framework of human interaction that reveals how we act in and perpetuate unhealthy roles—those of Victim, Rescuer, and Persecutor. I had certainly been stuck—typecast, as it were—in my default role during my latest drama. Fortunately, I later discovered

Introduction

the Drama Triangle's counterpart, the Winner's Triangle, which offers a way out of the dysfunctional cycle—a breakaway toward freedom and healthier relationships. Through it, I began to see what I had missed: that we don't have to stay stuck in our destructive relational dynamics.

These dynamics—the cycles of blame, avoidance, control, and healing—aren't just theoretical. They're embedded in the stories we live and the scriptures we love. Few biblical narratives illustrate this better than the story of Jonah. Beneath the story of prophet and fish is a deeply human drama: someone trying to outrun pain, deflect responsibility, and still wrestle with God's mercy.

This book is an invitation to reexperience Jonah's story through the lens of the Drama Triangle—not to reduce Scripture to a model but to offer you a new way of viewing your own story. If you've ever felt overwhelmed by the weight of conflict, betrayal, or spiritual confusion, my hope is that Jonah's journey—and mine—will help you discover that surrender to God is not giving up but waking up.

∼

"Jonah and the Whale" is arguably one of the first biblical stories that people learn in Sunday school or hear read from an illustrated children's Bible. It certainly sticks out as one of the most dramatic stories in the Bible. No doubt, a large fish swallowing a man adds to the climactic drama of any tale.

As a result, some believe that the book of Jonah is an allegory or a parable of sorts. This may be the case because it illustrates extreme characteristics that seem highly unlikely and even somewhat comical. Not the least of these is that Jonah just so happens to be saved from drowning through the timely "rescue" of a biological submarine.

Additionally, Jonah is one of the very few prophets whose audience responds with a quick and thorough repentance. In contrast, most of the prophets in Scripture are ignored or even killed for their messages. Furthermore, unlike most prophets, Jonah is

Introduction

not happy or relieved that his hearers repent and are saved from destruction. If you read the other Old Testament prophets, his reaction seems comically atypical. I mean, have you ever met a preacher who was dissatisfied or angry when his or her audience responded with agreement and immediate obedience? Taking this into account, Jonah is really not the godly man that one would assume a prophet of God to be.

Even the way his role shifts throughout the narrative raises questions about his eligibility as a biblical hero. Using the Drama and Winner's Triangles as a cast of characters, Jonah enters the stage as Victim, transitions to Persecutor, and then—corralled by God—becomes a reluctant Coach until the final act, when he defaults back to Victim, even suggesting that God is his Persecutor.

In essence, everything in the story of Jonah is so over the top and goes against the natural assumptions of its audience. It all seems unlikely and unbelievable, but that very well could be the point. In fact, the book of Jonah appears to be a literary juxtaposition, positioning its readers' assumptions with an opposing reality to serve as a rebuke for the hard-hearted and an invitation for those humble enough to surrender.

On the other hand, some argue that Jonah's story is a historical account—that he was a real prophet sent by God to Nineveh, swallowed by a sea creature, and spit out three days later. This is possible—at least the first part, anyway—as an actual man named Jonah is documented. In 2 Kings 14:25 (ESV), "Jonah the son of Amittai" is mentioned as a prophet from Gath-hepher, with a role in a well-documented historical context. So we have a prophet named Jonah, with a father named Amittai, from a place called Gath-hepher, in a specific time—the reign of Jeroboam II—taking specific action by speaking to the nation of Israel, which is being attacked by a historical enemy. It could not be more evident that there was a literal Jonah.

And so I am approaching this book from both perspectives—that Jonah's story is both historical and mythical. Jonah was a real prophet in the time of Jeroboam II, tasked with going to Nineveh. However, I also propose that parts of the story may have been

Introduction

accentuated to emphasize its deeper themes. Therefore, I want to view Jonah's narrative as both a literal history of events and a myth or moral history that conveys truths not to be forgotten.

I will often treat Jonah as a parody: a mythical or historical imitation/exaggeration of typical human behavior. I believe that the story functions primarily in this sense, allowing its author to make a larger, more meaningful point about the dynamics of human drama and the need for surrender.

For instance, throughout the years, I've noticed that in different seasons of my life, I've related to three distinct characters in the book: Jonah, the sailors, and the Ninevites. Each of these characters offers a moral sense of responsibility—a prescriptive example of how to behave in similar situations. This interpretation of Scripture is often referred to as *tropological*, offering a map from God that helps morally orient oneself.

For much of my life, I related to Jonah, running from my hurt and from what God was asking me to do. Like Jonah, I used vehicles—specifically, my anger—as a way to flee from my pain and avoid what God was inviting me into. Where Jonah boarded a ship bound for Tarshish, I relied on a deceptive sense of control. Where Jonah played the victim of the Assyrians, I played the victim of those who rejected or hurt me. But through Jonah's story, God helped me see the dramatic cycle I was stuck in and invited me into a posture of vulnerability, surrendering my hurt to him.

Later, I noticed how much I had in common with the sailors. I tried to rescue others, like Jonah, whom I perceived as powerless. In my frustration, I found myself stuck in a storm alongside those I was trying to save, offering mercy outside of God's will. I became passive when action was required and condoned behaviors that God didn't approve of. I was tolerating others rather than loving them.

In the end, I realized I was enabling others to avoid their responsibility and pain, while God was inviting me to surrender them to him.

Eventually, I recognized that I also shared much in common with the Ninevites. I had been, more often than I liked to admit,

Introduction

someone who used his power to manipulate and coerce others. This was often done unconsciously, yet also voluntarily. Through Jonah's story, God invited me, like he had invited the Ninevites, to surrender my power to him and trust his vision for my future.

∼

As I mentioned earlier, the moral sense I found in Jonah's story aligned with relational theories such as Karpman's Drama Triangle and Choy's Winner's Triangle. These theories didn't replace the biblical prescription but acted as a guide, helping me understand what surrender, vulnerability, and power look like practically in my life.

The pivotal point of the Drama Triangle is that we all relate to the roles of Victim, Rescuer, and Persecutor at different times, creating a kind of power play. According to Karpman, the game begins when the roles are established by the "actors" or anticipated by the "audience." There is no real drama unless there is a rotation in the roles. These role reversals create wasted energy and a lack of peace.[1] However, as we will see in the Winner's Triangle and the story of Jonah, vulnerable surrender is the key to breaking the cycle.[2]

My hope is to reintroduce readers to the story of Jonah through the perspectives of its characters, highlighting the dynamics of the Drama Triangle and the prescriptive posture God provides for each role, as seen in the Winner's Triangle.

Ultimately, Jonah's story is about surrendering one's hurt, control, and power:

- Jonah—the Victim—is invited to create a new future through the vulnerable surrender of his hurt.
- The Sailors—the Rescuers—are invited to surrender Jonah, whom they feel responsible for, to God's purposes.
- The Ninevites—the Persecutors—are invited to surrender their power and moral compass to God.

1. Karpman, "Fairy Tales," 39–43.
2. Choy, "Winner's Triangle," 40–46.

Introduction

As you read and reflect on your life in light of Jonah's drama, I invite you to consider surrendering your hurt, control, and power. Once you do, you break free of the cycle of relational drama and follow Christ into the Winner's Triangle.

THE DRAMA AND WINNER'S TRIANGLES

Before diving deeper into the story of Jonah, I believe it is necessary to provide you with a brief overview of the two important models I will be referencing: the Drama Triangle and the Winner's Triangle. These frameworks are essential for understanding the relational dynamics that will emerge as we explore Jonah's story.

The Drama Triangle

The Drama Triangle, created by Stephen Karpman in 1968, is a way to understand tricky and often unhealthy interactions in relationships. It identifies three roles that people play: Victim, Rescuer, and Persecutor.[3]

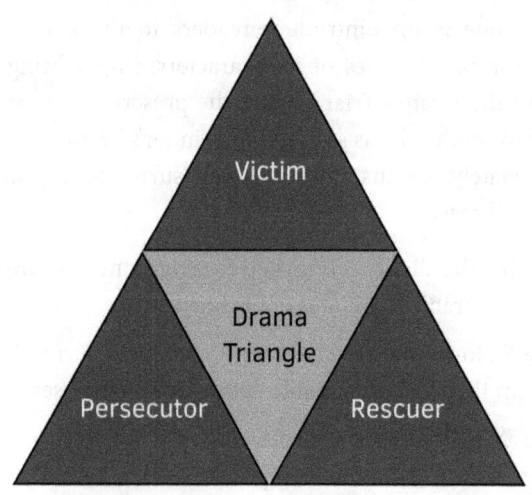

---

3. Karpman, "Fairy Tales," 39–43.

- Victim: This person feels helpless and powerless. They often feel sorry for themselves and look for someone to rescue them.
- Rescuer: This person tries to save others, even when it's not necessary. They often do too much for others because it makes them feel important.
- Persecutor: This person is coercive and critical and often blames others. They tend to dominate and put others down.

In relationships, these roles can rotate. For instance, someone who feels like a Victim might start blaming others, becoming a Persecutor. Or a Rescuer might feel unappreciated and start seeing themselves as a Victim. Each role depends on the others to keep the drama going: Victims need someone to rescue them, Rescuers need someone to save in order to feel needed, and Persecutors need someone to blame. These roles create a cycle that keeps everyone stuck in unhealthy patterns.

To break out of the cycle, the people involved must recognize the roles they have been playing and take responsibility for their actions. This involves communicating clearly, setting boundaries, and encouraging independence rather than fostering dependency. For example, a Rescuer, rather than solving someone else's problem for them, can support them as they try to solve it themselves. By breaking out of their roles, relationships become healthier and more balanced as the people involved move away from drama and toward mutual support and respect. Understanding and addressing these dynamics can help people build better, more fulfilling relationships.

The Winner's Triangle

The Winner's Triangle is a model created by Acey Choy in 1990 to foster healthier and more positive interactions in relationships. It's an alternative to Karpman's Drama Triangle and redefines the roles people play to promote growth and respect. In this model,

Introduction

the Victim becomes Vulnerable, the Rescuer becomes Caring, and the Persecutor becomes Assertive.[4]

- Vulnerable Creator: This role involves being honest and open about one's needs and weaknesses without feeling helpless. It's about taking responsibility for one's own life and seeking help in a constructive way.
- Caring Coach: Rather than taking over or enabling dependency, a caring person offers support and empathy, encouraging and coaching others to solve their own problems and develop their own strengths.
- Assertive Challenger: Instead of blaming or attacking others, someone who is assertive communicates their needs and boundaries clearly and respectfully.

By shifting from the negative roles of the Drama Triangle to these positive ones, individuals can break free from dysfunctional patterns. For example, someone who feels helpless can acknowledge their needs without giving up their power. A habitual helper can offer support in ways that empower others instead of making

4. Choy, "Winner's Triangle," 40–46.

Introduction

them dependent. And someone who usually coerces others can learn to express their needs without aggression. This approach leads to healthier relationships by encouraging open communication, responsibility, and mutual support. Adopting the principles of the Winner's Triangle promotes more balanced, respectful, and fulfilling interactions instead of drama.

∼

Now that we've covered an overview of the Drama and Winner's Triangles, I encourage you to explore these models further and keep them in mind as we delve into the book of Jonah. They will offer valuable insight as we unpack the relational dynamics within the narrative.

Part 1

Jonah
The Victim

1

On the Run

Jonah's Flight from God

"Where shall I go from your Spirit? Or where shall I flee from your presence?"

—Psalm 139:7 (ESV)

"Owning our story can be hard but not nearly as difficult as spending our lives running from it."

—Brené Brown, *The Gifts of Imperfection*

I WAS BORN IN the late seventies and grew up in the eighties, during which I encountered some of my first movies and toys from the *Star Wars* franchise. I vividly remember the release of *Return of the Jedi* and the excitement of collecting the first action figures. Despite this nostalgia, I find myself critiquing the *Star Wars* prequels and sequels for their perceived commercialism and lack of authenticity.

However, as I navigate my forties, I've grown to appreciate the latest trilogy, *Episodes VII–IX*, in a new light. A key factor in this shift is my ability to relate to Luke Skywalker, who wrestles with

Drowning in Drama

midlife disillusionment. He hasn't lost faith in the Force, but he has become disenchanted with the very institution he once revered—the Jedi Order. Like Jonah fleeing to Tarshish, Luke retreats to the Outer Rim, seeking refuge from both his past failures and his fears of what lies ahead. Fittingly, his X-wing serves as his escape pod, much like Jonah's ship—a vessel not just for physical retreat but also for evading the burdens of his calling.

I can so relate to Luke's painful disillusionment and his desire to run away from it all. For much of my life, I used anger as a way to cope with my fear and unwanted emotions. For me, anger was a safer emotion to identify with than fear. Anger at least gave me a temporary sense of power and control, while fear felt overwhelming and debilitating. In my pain, I often strove for control, and when my striving reached its limits, anger provided a temporary refuge by re-establishing a sense of comfort through intimidation. Obviously, this left a wake of collateral damage and abuse in my relationships.

I was a frightened young man using anger to escape my fear and hurt. Anger became my vehicle for running from unwanted emotions, particularly pain.

Interestingly, my anger came with a deception that prevented me from practicing vulnerability and surrender and, therefore, from finding peace and deeper connection. For the longest time, it never occurred to me that anger was a means of escaping my hurt and fear. Instead, it felt as if I was confronting my pain because I was willing to fight. The problem was that my anger was directed in the wrong way. I was fighting the wrong battle, running from my pain by avoiding the root causes and masking my escape with a false sense of power directed at others rather than at my fear.

In this way, I saw myself as a Victim who quickly turned into a Persecutor because I was afraid of the perceived powerlessness of vulnerability. Clearly, all of this stemmed from past anguish.

Similarly, while reading the book of Jonah, it is essential to understand that the main character has a genuine history of hurt that requires our attentive validation. It is unfair to draw conclusions about Jonah without first considering the context of his historical pain. Only then can we comprehend Jonah's hard heart and become aware of the possibility that we might currently share his calloused condition toward God and others.

∼

Jonah was a prophet of God in the nation of Israel, whose biggest enemy at the time was Assyria. Nineveh was the capital city of this hostile empire. As an example, in 2 Kings, we see the people of Israel suffering bitterly at the hands of their enemies, including the Assyrian Empire.

Let's take a look at Jonah's historical context, as presented in 2 Kings 14:23–27:

> In the fifteenth year of Amaziah son of Joash king of Judah, Jeroboam son of Jehoash king of Israel became king in Samaria, and he reigned forty-one years. He did evil in the eyes of the LORD and did not turn away from any of the sins of Jeroboam son of Nebat, which he had caused Israel to commit. He was the one who restored the boundaries of Israel from Lebo Hamath to the Dead Sea, in accordance with the word of the LORD, the God of Israel, spoken through his servant Jonah son of Amittai, the prophet from Gath Hepher.
>
> The LORD had seen how bitterly everyone in Israel, whether slave or free, was suffering; there was no one to help them. And since the LORD had not said he would blot out the name of Israel from under heaven, he saved them by the hand of Jeroboam son of Jehoash.

Did you catch the last two verses? Do you see how dire the situation is for Israel?

God takes note of the severe suffering of the Israelites. Everyone is in agony under Assyria's rule, including both the affluent and the poor. There is no hope for any of them unless God intervenes! In fact, the situation is so desperate that if God does not step in, they risk being wiped out as a people altogether. It would be fitting to imagine this episode for the people of Israel as a sort of ancient holocaust. Ironically, this crisis is accentuated by God

Drowning in Drama

having to reluctantly use the wicked king Jeroboam II to execute his plan for salvation.

Furthermore, when God asks Jonah to go and preach repentance to the city of Nineveh, he is essentially asking Jonah to face his most daunting enemy and deepest wounds. It is entirely possible—if not probable—that Jonah experienced personal trauma at the hands of the Assyrian Empire. Given this context, it is appropriate for us to allow our imaginations to explore the text more freely. Jonah most likely witnessed the brutal impact of his enemies on his people. No doubt he saw atrocities; he likely witnessed neighbors starving and struggling financially as the nation of Israel was threatened by the Assyrians. He may have had friends, and perhaps even family members, who bled out in battle. In short, it is safe to assume that Jonah and his family were profoundly affected by this national trauma.

Consider this caption from *Biblical Archaeology Review* describing an Assyrian artifact from the British Museum: "Assyrian headhunters gather their trophies. In a relief from Sennacherib's palace at Nineveh, two scribes, standing side by side . . . record the number of enemies slain in a campaign in southern Mesopotamia. Heads lie in a heap at their feet. . . ."[1]

Here are further corroborating archaeological accounts of Assyrian brutality:

> I flayed as many nobles as had rebelled against me [and] draped their skins over the pile [of corpses]; some I spread out within the pile, and others I erected on stakes upon the pile. . . . I flayed many right through my land [and] draped their skins over the walls. . . .
>
> I felled 50 of their fighting men with the sword, burned 200 captives from them, [and] defeated in a battle on the plain 332 troops. . . . With their blood, I dyed the mountain red like wool, [and] the rest of the ravines [and] torrents of the mountain swallowed. I carried off captives [and] possessions from them. . . . I burnt their adolescent boys [and] girls. . . .

---

1. Bleibtreu, "Grisly," 55.

On the Run

In strife and conflict, I besieged [and] conquered the city. I felled 3,000 of their fighting men with the sword.... I captured many troops alive: I cut off some of their arms [and] hands; I cut off of others their noses, ears, [and] extremities. I gouged out the eyes of many troops. I made one pile of the living [and] one of heads. I hung their heads on trees around the city.[2]

In riveting, gruesome detail, the king of Assyria documented and touted his extreme power and control over others. He presents himself as a ruthless authority figure who defines what is right simply by virtue of his power. The king embodies the mindset summarized by the motto "might equals right." His self-documentation of sadistic acts, along with the content of cruelty, suggests that the purpose of his power is to control the less powerful through fear, intimidation, and brutal violence. He is a terrorist, an oppressor, a coercive bully, and an abuser. In the Drama Triangle, he perfectly fulfills the role of Persecutor.

In light of all this, both Jonah and the nation of Israel have genuinely been victimized. However, Jonah is not powerless. God calls him to confront his enemies, personal pain, and historical trauma. This would be the modern-day equivalent of God asking a Western Christian to go to the Middle East and confront ISIS terrorists at the height of their power in 2014. Can you imagine? Is it any wonder that Jonah would choose to run from God and his purpose?

Here are some details we must consider in the story of Jonah:

- Jonah has valid hurt that God is trying to help him address and heal.
- Unaddressed and un-surrendered hurt can often lead us to try to escape our situations, as we see with Jonah; his unresolved pain and abhorrence of the idea of compassion shown to his nation's abusers causes him to run from God and others.
- He utilizes a vehicle to escape his hurt (an escape pod, for my fellow *Star Wars* fans). Jonah's vehicle of choice is a seagoing ship. Many people, like Jonah, choose to run from their pain.

2. Bleibtreu, "Grisly," 56.

Drowning in Drama

While most may not physically flee, they engage in avoidance behaviors and escapisms.

In Anna Lembke's book *Dopamine Nation*, she highlights this tendency: "We're all running from pain. . . . We'll do almost anything to distract ourselves from ourselves. Yet all this trying to insulate ourselves from pain seems only to make our pain worse."[3]

Brené Brown's research supports similar findings: "Pain is unrelenting. It will get our attention. Despite our attempts to drown in addiction, to physically beat it out of one another, to suffocate it with success and material trappings, or to strangle it with hate, pain will find a way to make itself known."[4] Likewise, Henri Nouwen identified this personal dynamic when he wrote in his 1996 book *The Inner Voice of Love*, "There is a great pain and suffering in the world. But the hardest pain to bear is your own."[5]

I can personally relate, as I have repeatedly found myself trying to escape my pain. As I mentioned earlier, I often used anger as a means to avoid my hurt. However, at one point, I also turned to lust as a way to escape feelings of loneliness and rejection. When I entered middle school, we moved to Massachusetts, just south of Boston, and I struggled to find friendship, connection, and any depth of real intimacy. My parents were involved and lovingly caring, but I felt I could not turn to them during this tumultuous time of adolescence.

In this season, I unconsciously concluded that lust, although an unwanted and shame-riddled substitute for intimacy, was a necessity. In doing so, I turned away from God's presence in search of relief through superficial connections. It took years, along with counseling, accountability, and my wife's loving but assertive challenges, to finally surrender and achieve lasting victory in these areas. It has been about seventeen years since lust has been a vehicle for my escape from the pain of loneliness and rejection. Praise God!

---

3. Lembke, *Dopamine*, 14.
4. Brown, *Gifts*, 47.
5. Nouwen, *Inner*, 13.

On the Run

Can you relate in any way? Perhaps not with anger or lust, but with choosing a vehicle to run from God and your pain. People choose many various dependencies and distractions to aid their escapism. Here are some modern behavioral patterns of medicating pain:

- Overeating
- Gambling
- Alcohol or drugs
- Prescription medications
- Television
- Video games
- Romance novels or pornography
- Social media
- Coffee
- Shopping
- Sex, lust, and masturbation
- Work
- Hurry and busyness

In reality, anything can become a getaway vehicle from our personal pain.

Consider your hurts; don't gloss over them. Allow both God and yourself to validate your feelings because they are undoubtedly real. Ignoring or dismissing your feelings only denies your own humanity and God's loving concern for you. Lovingly attend to your feelings so they don't overwhelm you and dictate your actions. Cross-reference your feelings with the truth by vulnerably sharing your hurts with God and trusted others. This integration of validated feelings and truth will lead to greater clarity and authenticity. Remember, while your feelings are real and deserving of validation, they may not always reflect the complete truth.

Drowning in Drama

ON THE RUN?

1. Do you find yourself often trying to escape and avoid pain?
2. Would you describe yourself as running from God, yourself, or others?
3. Would someone close to you say that you are dependent?
4. Would they say that you tend to use any of the preceding vehicles to self-medicate or numb your pain?
5. Is there anyone in your life you would have a hard time going to when in pain?
6. Do you ever feel victimized or powerless?

2

Repurposed Pain

How God Uses Pain as a Tool for Transformation and Growth

"But God saves those who suffer through their suffering; he gets them to listen through their pain."

—Job 36:15 (NCV)

"God whispers to us in our pleasures, speaks in our conscience, but shouts in our pain: it is his megaphone to rouse a deaf world."

—C. S. Lewis, *The Problem of Pain*

On a family vacation when my kids were very young, my nephew got sick with a common stomach bug. It was likely one of his first experiences of being miserably ill. He was up all night vomiting and couldn't find the relief that usually comes after clearing the stomach. At one point, after several bouts of vomiting, he declared aloud, "Why does God hate me? I prayed twice, and he still hasn't healed me!"

My nephew captured the struggle we often face with pain: Why does a good God allow us to endure suffering?

Drowning in Drama

Similarly, when reflecting on the most painful times in my life, the question I most often found myself asking was "Why?" I have repeatedly sought to understand the purpose behind God's allowing me and others to suffer.

At first, my pursuit of pain's purpose was primarily a search for resolution—to change the uncomfortable situation I found myself in. But I noticed that the continuation of pain prodded a necessary, more extensive examination of my soul. Persistent pain uncovers areas in our inner lives that also require reflection, critique, and possible adjustment.

In other words, pain that was not quickly resolved pushed me to examine things from a different perspective or at a deeper level of consciousness. In this sense, persistent pain can be reframed as a possible grace, revealing deep-seated issues within the soul and ultimately leading to answers.

∼

In the story of Jonah, we find God using a storm, a sea creature, and the oppressive sun to progressively probe Jonah's calloused heart and reveal his hurt, unforgiveness, and lack of mercy toward others whom God loves.

Interestingly, in all these moments of pain, God allows Jonah's discomfort to become more acute. The storm grows more perilous. Jonah's flesh deteriorates in the dark depths of the sea creature's belly. The sun becomes unbearably scorching. These insufferable pains and fears offer a curious hope by probing deeper into the wound, as though searching for a foreign object causing infection and disease. In other words, God sometimes uses pain as an investigative process to uncover the source of our soul's problems and, therefore, bring to light their remedies. This certainly seems to be the case for Jonah.

In chapter one, the storm worsens to the point at which even the sailors are terrified of total loss. In chapter two, Jonah is in the belly of the great fish, sinking into the depths and withering away, both physically and emotionally. We can imagine his body wasting

Repurposed Pain

away due to the corrosive effects of the creature's stomach acid as he is slowly being digested. Talk about a slow, painful way to die!

Surprisingly, it is in this severe probe of pain that Jonah finally directs his heart toward God in prayer. He says, "When my life was ebbing away, I remembered you, LORD, and my prayer rose to you, to your holy temple" (Jonah 2:7).

The depth of pain illustrated in Jonah's being physically digested aligns with the archetypal imagery of a descent into hell. This pain becomes unnatural, unbearable, and yet oddly purposeful, providing the necessary awareness for a change of heart and behavior. It presents the possibility of not only death but also a kind of resurrection. For example, Jonah admits that his attention is redirected toward God and his presence when he has finally had enough of his discomforting condition.

Pain does that—it is both a necessary attention-grabber and a motivator. It has the ability to capture our focus like nothing else can. Pain often brings a higher consciousness with its own brand of wisdom. It offers a distinct awareness and motivation that takes over when the stimulant of pleasure has reached its limit of influence.

I have often reflected on this principle of pleasure and pain—what the Bible calls "blessing" and "curse." These positive and negative incentives both pull and push us to seek the highest virtues of life, helping us grow and achieve at our best.

I know I have personally benefited not only from the carrot before me but also from the stick behind me. You too?

~

This powerful theme is illustrated in *The Giver* by Lois Lowry. If you haven't read the book, you've most likely seen the movie. (I highly recommend reading or watching it again.) In the story, we see Jonas, the main character, selected to become a recipient of human memories so that he can serve his community in an advisory role.

Sadly, his community has intentionally forgotten the painful memories of the past and, in doing so, has unintentionally lost the

Drowning in Drama

pleasures of true humanness. Jonas's training for this role involves rejecting the medication designed to numb him and the other community members. Unlike the rest of the community, he is called to live on the edge, courageously receiving both joyous and painful memories, enabling him to advise the community elders through his ability to "see beyond."[1]

Ultimately, Jonas—like Jonah, who interestingly shares a similar name—is invited to surrender himself vulnerably to pain as a form of education or preparation. This leads him to a new awareness and equips him to serve others prophetically, bringing freedom, real peace, and a fuller sense of humanity to his context.

∼

In light of all this, it becomes clear that God is concerned with something more profound in people—something more than just our physical or emotional contentment. God seems to leverage physical and emotional discomfort and pain (with an agenda of love) to accomplish a deeper work of virtue. In short, suffering can mysteriously produce significant meaning if we allow it. Or as author Thomas Moore notes, "The soul apparently needs amorous sadness. It is a form of consciousness that brings its own unique wisdom."[2]

Ultimately, God seems to be working to realize some virtue or God-like characteristic in both Jonah and us—something more highly prized and glorious than we could imagine. In this, we see that God is not the author of pain but rather an alchemist of the soul. He refuses to waste the raw materials of one's environment, instead creatively orchestrating a crucible of context—a refining process that includes pain and suffering—to bring about something more precious and glorious in those He loves.

---

1. Lowry, *Giver*, 120.
2. Moore, *Care*, 12.

REPURPOSING PAIN

1. Have you ever been in such pain that you thought God was displeased with you, despised you, or was simply absent?
2. Do you ever struggle with why God would allow you to go through pain?
3. Have you ever felt like God was either the cause of your pain (sadistic) or rather a careless bystander (aloof)?
4. Do you ever question why God would have you do something that you don't like, such as being vulnerable?
5. Have you ever wondered why God allows suffering?

3

Passing Peace

The Deceptive, Parasitic Nature of False Peace and Its Detrimental Damage

"'Peace, peace,' they say, when there is no peace."
—JEREMIAH 6:14

"I get those fleeting, beautiful moments of inner peace and stillness—and then the other 23 hours and 45 minutes of the day, I'm a human trying to make it through in this world."
—ELLEN DEGENERES

IN AUGUST OF 1991, New England experienced one of its costliest hurricanes. This storm, called "Bob," with reported winds of more than a hundred miles an hour, directly hit the area where I lived, leaving downed trees, power outages, and damaged buildings. The memories I have of this storm are the kind that stick with you. It wasn't the destruction or the severity of the wind that was so memorable, but rather the contrast of a quiet, temporary, false peace that I witnessed in the eye of the storm.

Passing Peace

I was fourteen years old and remember running out in the storm with my dad, mom, and brother to witness the eye of the hurricane. The wind was violently blowing in one direction and then suddenly died. The sun appeared, and an unsettling peace came over the scene. We knew it was fleeting, but we were drawn to it nonetheless. Almost as suddenly as the eye passed over our area, the opposite end of the storm hit.

The real devastation in my area came from the opposing winds, separated by the false peace of the hurricane's eye. Trees that had been forced to bend in one direction were now pressed the opposite way, and some were uprooted altogether. For my family and others in my community, the eye was a temporary peace that drew us out, exposing us to an even more precarious danger. The eye was indeed peaceful but also temporary and, therefore, deceptively dangerous. It could have been called a "fake peace."

Likewise, when I sought to medicate my pain of loneliness and desire for intimacy through lust, I can say that it worked—temporarily. I did experience peace! I felt a high that offered me a personal and isolated contentment... until the shame came. However, the peace I experienced was fragile and fleeting, like a puff of smoke, a bubble, or the release of dopamine in my body. My sense of peace was temporal. Too often, it left me with a quick satiation, only to be followed by a more ravenous appetite for something more substantial and sustainable.

It was like eating something delicious but devoid of nutritional value, ultimately triggering an aching emptiness that morphed into a greater craving.

Like Jonah asleep in the ship, I experienced peace as long as I could quiet my conscience. However, for me, quieting my conscience required a more complex behavioral formula than simply sleeping. I constantly strove to redirect my mind, searching for a metaphorical image of ideal intimacy to lust after, and thus numb my loneliness through distraction. Of course, the solution I employed brought even greater shame. Like the eye of a hurricane, my attempt at peace was short-lived, fake, and false. The storm raged on, often more dangerously than before. My pursuit of peace became an addictive cycle.

How about you?

- Have you ever sown the wind and reaped the whirlwind?
- Have you noticed how much of what you do is for the purpose of finding pleasure and avoiding pain?
- Have you ever caught yourself searching for some semblance of peace?

~

Let's look back at the story of Jonah. In his attempt to flee from God, Jonah boards a ship to Tarshish (modern-day Spain), somewhere near the ends of the earth. He is trying to escape God and his call, seeking peace for his troubled conscience.

Jonah falls asleep on the boat, finding temporary rest through exhaustion from his weary conscience. However, in both his love for Jonah and his love for the Ninevites, God sends a storm to disrupt Jonah's pursuit of personal peace. The storm intensifies, threatening the lives of everyone on board. Ultimately, Jonah is awakened by the ship's captain, who is desperate to understand their loss of peace and the reason for the storm.

Let's look at Jonah 1:1–6:

> The word of the LORD came to Jonah son of Amittai: "Go to the great city of Nineveh and preach against it, because its wickedness has come up before me." But Jonah ran away from the LORD and headed for Tarshish. He went down to Joppa, where he found a ship bound for that port. After paying the fare, he went aboard and sailed for Tarshish to flee from the LORD.
>
> Then the LORD sent a great wind on the sea, and such a violent storm arose that the ship threatened to break up. All the sailors were afraid and each cried out

Passing Peace

to his own god. And they threw the cargo into the sea to lighten the ship.

But Jonah had gone below deck, where he lay down and fell into a deep sleep. The captain went to him and said, "How can you sleep? Get up and call on your god! Maybe he will take notice of us so that we will not perish."

Strangely, Jonah does experience a brief sense of calm, and notably, his temporary peace coincides with a larger brewing storm. This is rather odd but often goes unnoticed.

- How can Jonah be experiencing both a storm and peace at the same time?
- Why is his attempt at peace short-lived?
- Why does his peace and rest coincide with his companions' growing anxiety and disturbance?
- Why is Jonah's peace intentionally and progressively disrupted by God through the captain?

Why? Because Jonah's superficial peace has come at the expense of others. In this specific situation, Jonah's peace comes at the cost of the Ninevites, who could experience peace with God—and therefore with other nations—if only Jonah would deliver the word God wants him to share. Likewise, Israel could find significant peace with their enemy, the Assyrians. And subsequently, the captain and sailors of the ship would be free from the storm sent to frustrate Jonah's attempt to flee. In short, others have lost their sense of peace due to Jonah's independent, perfunctory quest for his own peace.

The kind of peace Jonah is pursuing can be deemed *temporal*—a peace that will not last because it is derived from the peace of those around him. This kind of peace operates in a parasitic way. It comprises an individual achieving peace by hijacking and taking advantage of others without their consent. In this way, peace has limits and is inherently temporary.

This kind of peace is problematic because it singularly focuses on the individual without concern for others and, therefore, disrupts the individual's relationship with those same others. That is inherently why it does not last! Peace sought solely for an individual at the expense of others is not a peace that will or should endure.

This may strike a nerve with some of you, but I would nonetheless like to offer an archetypal vampire as an allegorical image of a Victim who settles for temporal peace. A vampire hungers for life—or peace—at the cost of others. The vampire, once a Victim, now seeks peace through power and charm, seducing and manipulating others to meet its valid needs through invalid means. It drains peace from others yet never truly satisfies its own hunger for inner tranquility.

As I described earlier in my cycle of lust, I am grieved to admit that I can relate to this miserable state of parasitical peace. Like Jonah, I have held others hostage. I have used others as my source of peace instead of turning to God. I have settled for temporal peace in place of perfect peace.

TEMPORARY PEACE

1. Have your attempts to find peace left you with a sense of shame?
2. Have you ever noticed the fragility of peace when using something to medicate your pain?
3. Do you find those around you disrupting your attempts at peace?
4. Do you catch yourself relying on something other than God to give you a sense that all is well in the world?

4

The Transformative Power of Vulnerability

Surrendering Our Fear and Hurt

"[For] Christ's sake, I delight in weaknesses, in insults, in hardships, in persecutions, in difficulties. For when I am weak, then I am strong."
—2 CORINTHIANS 12:10

"Vulnerability is the birthplace of innovation, creativity, and change."
—BRENÉ BROWN

AS I MENTIONED IN the introduction of this book, my wife and I experienced an upheaval like none other. Amid the swirling chaos of the storm, I witnessed my wife choose God and his invitation to be courageously vulnerable. What began as a quiet effort to seek justice eventually led her to speak out, not only for herself but also for others who had suffered in silence. Her decision was gut-wrenching and costly. She exposed herself to scrutiny and criticism. But her vulnerability, I would soon learn, wasn't weakness.

Drowning in Drama

It was a prophetic act—a critique not just of what happened but of the system that allowed it to keep happening.

Since then, many friends have asked me what it was like as a husband to watch his wife make such a difficult decision and walk through the repercussions of it with her. I have found the best way to frame my experience is through an unusual story in the book of Judges.

In chapters 19–21 of Judges is a story I never thought or hoped I would be able to relate to—a story about a Levite and one of his wives. The Levite is traveling home after fetching his wife and comes to the Israelite city of Gibeah. In that town, men (reminiscent of those in Sodom and Gomorrah) gang-rape the wife, and as a result, she dies. The Levite then takes her body home and methodically dismembers it, sending her in pieces throughout the land of Israel. This gruesome act triggers a civil war to address the tolerated injustice within the nation of Israel. Truly gruesome!

You may ask, what does this story have to do with witnessing *my* wife's vulnerability as a Victim? Well, much like the Levite, I had to observe my wife suffering wrongs at the hands of God's people, who should have known better. Subsequently, I had to look on as a death of sorts took place in her—an emotional and spiritual death—as a direct result of this mistreatment and betrayal. If that wasn't enough, I had to watch as she, in a way, dissected herself, publicly exposing her wounded parts to the community in hopes of drawing attention to the wrongs that God no longer wanted to be tolerated among his people. I also had to watch as many who knew about it remained silent.

All courageous Victims, like my wife, who choose sacrificial vulnerability in the face of their hurt, create new possibilities for needed change. They endure death at the hands of their oppressors and yet choose to expose their pain. They allow the vulnerable parts of themselves to be analyzed, scrutinized, and then publicized throughout their community for all to see. Their hope is that people will share in their visceral shock at such wrongs and work to correct what has been wrongfully permitted.

The Transformative Power of Vulnerability

How about you?

- Have you ever noticed how a Victim's vulnerability provides the necessary motivation for transformation in a community?
- Have you ever witnessed the sacrificial courage it takes for a Victim to go public?
- Has a Victim's vulnerability ever moved you? Did you notice the direction in which you and others were moved?

∼

Let's get back to Jonah. It's important to remember that God is giving Jonah a similar invitation to trust him, to surrender, and to choose vulnerability. Jonah is a Victim who can vulnerably surrender to God and the Ninevites, thereby bringing an opportunity for much-needed change.

Instead of remaining in victimhood, Jonah initially submits to God's invitation to choose vulnerability. This is exemplified first by his decision on the ship to stop running and suggest that he be thrown overboard. Second, he stopped looking to the sailors to rescue him—another reluctant capitulation to making himself vulnerable.

Let's take a look at Jonah 1:11–15:

> The sea was getting rougher and rougher. So they asked him, "What should we do to you to make the sea calm down for us?"
>
> "Pick me up and throw me into the sea," he replied, "and it will become calm. I know that it is my fault that this great storm has come upon you."
>
> Instead, the men did their best to row back to land. But they could not, for the sea grew even wilder than before. Then they cried out to the LORD, "Please, LORD, do not let us die for taking this man's life. Do not hold us accountable for killing an innocent man, for you, LORD, have done as you pleased." Then they took Jonah and threw him overboard, and the raging sea grew calm.

Drowning in Drama

In this passage, we see Jonah finally choosing to submit, though not necessarily surrendering to vulnerability. He reluctantly stops trying to save himself by his own power and allows himself to be put in a powerless situation, trusting God in a vulnerable way. He essentially identifies the storm as the result of his running from God and God's will. Jonah correctly surmises that if he would only surrender and stop running, the storm would cease. He suggests that the sailors throw him overboard into the turbulent sea.

Here we see Jonah stop looking to the sailors as his Rescuers. This is a small yet reluctant step in the right direction. He acknowledges that the sailors cannot keep rescuing him, as it will cost them their lives. They cannot continue enabling him to run from God if they want the storm to end.

However, it's important to note that Jonah is a reluctant participant in this particular vulnerability. He still prefers victimhood. In verse 12, Jonah says, "I know that it is my fault," yet he places the responsibility on the sailors to "rescue" him one last time by suggesting they be the ones to throw him overboard. He's choosing a kind of suicide by martyrdom, effectively offering himself to the sailors to be killed. In this, we see Jonah's hesitation in fully surrendering. He opts for submission over surrender, asking the crew to throw him off the ship—an act he could have done himself, which would have saved the sailors from their guilt and misplaced sense of responsibility.

As I shared in an earlier chapter, Jonah is a Victim with a real history of hurt. He enters the Drama Triangle as the default Victim, dreading that God would be gracious to his Persecutors, the Assyrians. And so he chooses to run from his responsibility to vulnerably surrender his pain and fear to God. He fearfully avoids using his power to change the drama he and others are experiencing.

Here we see the common theme that motivates most Victims in the Drama Triangle: fear driven by hurt. For Jonah, his specific fear is that God will be exactly who Jonah knows him to be: loving and gracious. Jonah says, "Isn't this what I said, Lord, when I was still at home. . . ? I knew that you are a gracious and compassionate God" (Jonah 4:2).

The Transformative Power of Vulnerability

Let's jump ahead in the story to look deeper into this fear, which is realized when the Ninevites repent. Read Jonah 3:10—4:3:

> When God saw what they did and how they [the Ninevites] turned from their evil ways, he relented and did not bring on them the destruction he had threatened. . . .
> But to Jonah this seemed very wrong, and he became angry. He prayed to the LORD, "Isn't this what I said, LORD, when I was still at home? That is what I tried to forestall by fleeing to Tarshish. I knew that you are a gracious and compassionate God, slow to anger and abounding in love, a God who relents from sending calamity. Now, LORD, take away my life, for it is better for me to die than to live."

I think it's important to note a few things: Although Jonah starts off as a Victim, he goes through a process of vulnerable submission, first by offering himself to be thrown overboard and then more fully by agreeing to go to Nineveh. His submission creates new opportunities for better relationships between Israel, Nineveh, and God. But he also later transitions into the role of Persecutor, as witnessed by his ire when Nineveh repents and is subsequently not destroyed. Ultimately, Jonah moves from Victim to Persecutor because of his hurt-driven fear, revealing his preference for a world without the Assyrian Empire altogether. God invites him to become vulnerable and challenge his Persecutors, and while Jonah does so, it is grudgingly. Sadly, in chapter 4, we see that Jonah would rather see God destroy the Ninevites.

Additionally, in Jonah 3:3, we should notice Jonah's heart. He perceives God's graciousness to the Ninevites as a form of persecution toward *him*. Essentially, Jonah views himself as a Victim of God's goodness to his enemies. He essentially tells God, "You're doing me wrong, so I might as well die at your hands." He gives God an ultimatum: "It's either them or me!" Jonah mistakenly frames God as his personal Persecutor.

This is the sad cycle and nature of the Drama Triangle. People start in a default role—whether Victim, Rescuer, or Persecutor—and all roles compete to become the greatest Victim. The reversals

Drowning in Drama

that occur in these roles, as each tries to claim the most victimhood, create a toxic drama of unhealthy relationship dynamics.

For Jonah, he starts as a Victim of the Ninevites but later becomes their Persecutor, only to revert back to the Victim role once again. However, this time, he weaves God into the drama, seeing God as his Persecutor for showing grace to the Ninevites.

Ultimately, the only solution to escape the toxic drama I've just illustrated is through continued surrender. For Jonah, who defaults to the Victim role, this surrender must be to God, recognizing his personal vulnerability and choosing to not only submit but to continually surrender to God.

A Victim always has the door of vulnerability and surrender available. It is the single greatest power a Victim can exercise! However, too often, we confuse vulnerability with liability and struggle, as Jonah does.

～

A story that is helpful in capturing the dynamics I've mentioned in this chapter is Disney's *Encanto*. If you are the parent or grandparent of young kids, you've probably already seen this meaningful movie. If not, I suggest you watch it, as it introduces the Drama Triangle, family systems theory, and most importantly, the power of vulnerability to transform a community.

In this story, the characters discover that Maribel Madrigal, the only member of a magical family *without* magical gifts, does indeed have a valuable contribution to make—one that comes from her weakness. Her power ultimately lies in her apparent lack of magical power, which leads to her willingness to be vulnerable. Sadly, her family is too afraid of such vulnerability because it brings unwanted exposure. The Madrigals implicitly see Maribel's vulnerability as a threat to their status. Yet through her courageous and continued willingness to be vulnerable, she creates new possibilities for both her family and her community.

In the final scene, the Madrigal family celebrates Maribel's weakness as her true power, leading them into a much-needed

The Transformative Power of Vulnerability

renewal. Uncle Bruno succinctly summarizes the story when he tells Maribel, "You're the real gift, kid. Let us in!"[1] In short, Maribel's vulnerability ultimately addresses the biggest danger everyone was afraid to acknowledge: the underlying brokenness in the family system and community.

SURRENDERING TO GOD AND HIS INVITATION TO VULNERABILITY

1. Does vulnerability seem only to be a liability to you?
2. Would you describe your entrance into vulnerability as a reluctant submission or a surrender to God?
3. What does God's invitation to being vulnerable stir up in you?
4. What possibilities are you leaving on the table by not being willing to be vulnerable?

---

1. Bush, *Encanto*.

5

True Peace

The Peace That Abides When in Harmony with God, Self, and Community

"You will keep in perfect peace those whose minds are steadfast, because they trust in you."

—Isaiah 26:3

"We are not at peace with others because we are not at peace with ourselves, and we are not at peace with ourselves because we are not at peace with God."

—(attributed to) Thomas Merton

I AM A LATE Gen-Xer who likes *Star Wars* a little too much, so I'm unapologetically going to use another example from the *Star Wars* universe. Not a problem, I'm sure, for some like-minded readers.

In the 2016 *Rogue One* story, we are introduced to a new character who is rich in significance to the overall *Star Wars* mythology: Chirrut Imwe, a blind monk of the Force. He moves through life with an inner tranquility that seems to result from his literal blind trust in an unseen power. Chirrut unabashedly relies

True Peace

on the Force to guide and direct his fight for what is right and good. He knows he belongs to this great power and abides in it, allowing it to focus his attention and abilities as needed. This is exemplified in his repeated mantra throughout the movie: "I am one with the Force. The Force is with me."[1] In short, Chirrut demonstrates peace by practicing the presence of the Force, especially in the midst of chaotic crises.

I fall short of this amazing sense of belonging, tranquility, and peace. However, I have at times found that true peace comes as a result of vulnerably surrendering myself to God. An example is when my wife began to sense it was time to go public about the misconduct she had suffered.

I personally wrestled with this decision because it meant stepping out of the boat, leaving our institution's family system and its cultural, implicit bias that I had always been a part of. It required being willing to confront the powers that be in a way I knew would be seen as scandalous. As Brené Brown says, it meant "braving the wilderness."[2] Sadly, I probably cared too much about what my peers thought of me and my wife.

That said, I needed to hear from God and receive the kind of personal peace that only comes from his presence and promises. In this struggle, I found myself repeatedly returning to the book of Ruth. In this short story, I sensed God settling me with the insight that, like Naomi—who asked to be called Mara (meaning bitterness)—my wife needed to publicly identify with her bitterness. Not only for her own good but also for the good of the community, she had to vulnerably expose the truth through a visceral disclosure of her hurt. At that point, I realized that my role wasn't to rescue but to coach through the difficult, scandalous process of uncovering our institution's neglected responsibilities.

Just as Ruth uncovered Boaz's responsibility—which, according to biblical law, was to act as a kinsman-redeemer—my wife had to uncover our institution's failures with the hope of bringing peace to the larger community. Ultimately, despite my

1. Edwards, *Rogue One*.
2. Brown, *Braving*, 41.

misgivings, I surrendered to what I came to believe was God's work, not simply ours.

God's peace and his word consoled me, bringing me confidence in his will. It may sound like a paradox, but this godly serenity confronted and unsettled the misplaced security I had placed in my leaders and community. It also grounded me with a sense of self-efficacy—a differentiation, or authentic belonging, to myself. In essence, it gave me the ability to maintain my own identity, emotions, and thoughts while staying emotionally connected to others. It allowed me to cultivate healthy independence and interdependence, preventing the blurred boundaries and emotional over-reliance that come with enmeshment. Most succinctly, this surrender brought me a peace with God as well as with myself.

From this place of belonging to God and myself, I could confront—with newfound love and honor—those people I had lost respect for. In short, I had to surrender to God and his presence, which brought a perfecting peace. I needed to rest with a repentant and humble heart, waiting for God's presence to secure me. Only then could I be whole enough to belong to my true self. And only after finding peace with myself could I step into the authority to courageously contend for possible peace with others.

How about you?

- Are you in need of God's presence and promise that secures?
- Are you experiencing anxiety because you have not truly belonged to your authentic self?
- Are you personally secure enough to confront the wrongs of others with real confidence in God's direction and the authentic integrity of a heart that loves your enemies?
- Can you relate to this kind of perfecting peace?

∼

True Peace

Let's go back to Jonah 1:15—2:2 and look at the peace Jonah begins to experience:

> Then they took Jonah and threw him overboard, and the raging sea grew calm. At this the men greatly feared the LORD, and they offered a sacrifice to the LORD and made vows to him.
>
> Now the LORD provided a huge fish to swallow Jonah, and Jonah was in the belly of the fish three days and three nights.
>
> From inside the fish Jonah prayed to the LORD his God. He said:
>
> "In my distress I called to the LORD, and he answered me. From deep in the realm of the dead I called for help, and you listened to my cry."

Did you catch verse 15? "They took Jonah and threw him overboard, and the raging sea grew calm."

Right after Jonah takes a step of submission, the storm subsides, and he experiences an outward symbol of order replacing chaos. This peace—the calming of the raging storm—signifies his initial alignment with God and God's will. Nature serenely echoes Jonah's submission to God and God's love for both Jonah and everyone else involved in the drama.

However, not everything is perfect or complete, as the ship and sailors are slipping away. It becomes evident that Jonah is now in a deep, isolated environment with no apparent hope on the horizon. Let's take a moment to place ourselves in Jonah's predicament. On the one hand, he likely feels some relief and comfort, knowing he is now right with God and the sailors. On the other hand, he must also feel a profound sense of concern, facing abandonment at sea with no visible salvation in sight. Surely, there is some anxiety, or possibly relief, over the real risk of drowning.

Interestingly, the peace Jonah experiences coincides with his circumstances becoming more dire. Why?

Because Jonah is being weaned from his reliance on temporal peace. He is suddenly severed from the source of his temporal

Drowning in Drama

peace—the sailors: his co-dependents, his Rescuers, those he has used to enable his attempts at self-salvation.

It is through the process of experiencing God's perfecting peace that Jonah learns to quietly trust in God and his gracious goodness, which will faithfully emerge from the deep unknown. From beneath the surface of what seems possible, God provides Jonah with the reassurance of salvation: a sea monster—an unpleasant yet saving grace!

Furthermore, now that Jonah has made peace with God through submission, he will be challenged to reconcile with his authentic self—the reluctant part of him that, for now, is only willing to do the bare minimum for God. In other words, having made peace with God, Jonah is now confronted with the inner conflict between the parts of himself. The divergent aspects of his nature will be challenged in hopes of achieving greater wholeness by the part of him that has aligned with God.

This confrontation symbolically occurs through an archetypal image of death: Jonah being swallowed by a great fish. He must slowly die to his own will, corralled into facing his calloused heart, which remains hardened toward God and others.

~

Inside the fish, Jonah continues to pray, ending his psalm with, "But I, with shouts of grateful praise, will sacrifice to you. What I have vowed I will make good. I will say, 'Salvation comes from the LORD.'" (Jonah 2:9).

Notice how Jonah's prayer captures this idea of being made whole. He states, "What I have vowed I will make good." Jonah is finally becoming his whole self. He is resolving to take ownership of his responsibility; he is confronting his power and prerogative to relate to God and others through continued vulnerability.

Subsequently, this peace with God and wholeness of self enables Jonah to vulnerably face his history of hurt in Nineveh. In chapter 3, we see that God's word comes to Jonah a second time. God again asks Jonah to go to Nineveh and confront his enemies and trauma with vulnerability. This time, having made peace with God and himself, Jonah is more prepared. Though reluctant, he is now ready to proclaim repentance among the Ninevites.

Let's take a look at Jonah 3:1–4:

> Then the word of the LORD came to Jonah a second time: "Go to the great city of Nineveh and proclaim to it the message I give you."
>
> Jonah obeyed the word of the LORD and went to Nineveh. Now Nineveh was a very large city; it took three days to go through it. Jonah began by going a day's journey into the city, proclaiming, "Forty more days and Nineveh will be overthrown."

Notice verse 3: Jonah obeys the word of the Lord yet reluctantly confronts his hurt, his enemy, and his fear. Jonah participates in God's will for perfecting peace—a peace not only for Jonah and the sailors but also for Israel and even Israel's enemy, the Ninevites.

Amazingly, God is also working to perfect peace between himself and the Ninevites!

This is truly a perfect peace—a true peace—an alignment of all parties in proper order with God himself. This peace is a hierarchical, reciprocal belonging to one another—a relationship of relating to and partnering with one another.

In light of all this, you can probably sense that true peace seems to have more than one dimension. In fact, perfect peace appears to have at least three relational dimensions. It begins with peace from and with God, then moves toward personal wholeness and security within oneself, and finally proposes a possible peace with others for partnership.

How about you?

- Does this description of true peace resonate with you?
- Do your experiences of both peace and turmoil fit into this more nuanced understanding of temporal and true peace?

Drowning in Drama

Brené Brown demonstrates these three dimensions of true peace in her book *Braving the Wilderness*. She reflects on her research, stating:

> As I dug deeper into true belonging, it became clear that it's not something we achieve or accomplish with others; it's something we carry in our heart. Once we belong thoroughly to ourselves and believe thoroughly in ourselves, true belonging is ours. Belonging to ourselves means being called to stand alone—to brave the wilderness of uncertainty, vulnerability, and criticism. And with the world feeling like a political and ideological combat zone, this is remarkably tough. We seem to have forgotten that even when we're utterly alone, we're connected to one another by something greater than group membership, politics, and ideology—that we're connected by love and the human spirit.[3]

Brown presents this belonging through love as a vision of peace for all. She later clarifies in her book that true belonging with oneself and others must be grounded in something greater than the self or others. She describes the absence of this larger connection as a spiritual crisis.[4]

For me—and hopefully for you too—this ultimate connection is God. Like Jonah, I propose that we can only experience true peace with ourselves and others by first experiencing peace with and from God.

PARTNERING WITH GOD'S PERFECTING OF PEACE

1. Will you let God perfect a true peace in you?
2. Have you made peace with God by surrendering to his vision and presence?

---

3. Brown, *Braving*, 36–37.
4. See chapter 3 of *Braving the Wilderness* by Brené Brown.

3. What would it look like for you to partner with God by making peace with your authentic self?

4. What's holding you back from lovingly confronting others?

6

Enduring the Process
Salvation, Restoration, and Surrender

"[Continue] to work out your salvation with fear and trembling, for it is God who works in you to will and to act in order to fulfill his good purpose."
—PHILIPPIANS 2:12–13

"Salvation is from our side a choice, from the divine side it is a seizing upon, an apprehending, a conquest by the Most High God."
—A. W. TOZER, *THE PURSUIT OF MAN*

AS I'VE CONFESSED, I habitually utilized anger as a means to hide from God and my fear. Only after substantial storms had accrued did I finally abandon my intimidating behavior—my attempted vehicle for salvation and personal deliverance. I would like to suggest that life got immediately better with my surrender; however, that would be a lie. As you can imagine, matters became complicated, unpredictable, disorienting, and therefore, substantially worse.

Around 2007, my wife and I experienced one of our most difficult seasons as a couple. To be honest, I think both of us

Enduring the Process

wondered if our marriage would survive. We had recently been assigned to a new location and had three young kids, all under the age of six. Our individual issues were rising to the surface, and my anger—used to shield me from my fear of not being enough—raged. Fortunately, we had the opportunity to spend two weeks in the mountains of Colorado, receiving timely counseling in the hope of finding a breakthrough. During those two weeks, as we processed years of baggage and hurt, we shared an experience that came to symbolize our marriage journey.

It all came together for me when our counselor encouraged us to take some time outdoors together. We were in the beautiful town of Buena Vista, Colorado, at the headwaters of the Arkansas River, surrounded by "fourteeners," mountain peaks that reach fourteen thousand feet or higher. We chose to go for a hike and came across a smaller mountain, about ten thousand feet in elevation. Initially, the trails were clearly marked, with views of the town and valley below. As we began the hike, we formed expectations based on what we could see—expectations that quickly proved incorrect.

About halfway up, we realized that what we had thought was the summit was only a false peak. When we reached it, we saw that the true summit awaited just beyond the alpine zone, high in elevation and covered with snow. We were not prepared! If we had known this at the beginning of the hike, we might not have committed to the process. Exhausted and disheartened, we discussed whether we should turn back or push forward, staying true to our initial resolve.

We decided to go for it and, eventually, made it to the summit. We took an amazing picture, and with a sense of real accomplishment, we descended, celebrating our journey together. Later that week, I mentioned to my wife and our counselor how this hike felt symbolic of our decision to confront the difficult issues in our marriage. Just like the hike, we had begun our marriage journey not knowing we were unprepared for the long process ahead. We knew it would be hard, but we hadn't anticipated how it would stretch us beyond our confidence in our own abilities.

Drowning in Drama

Through this, I came to see firsthand that submitting our plans and timing to God is only the first step in embracing the journey of surrender. For us, deliverance and restoration came not as a single moment of breakthrough but as a painful process—one to be endured rather than instantly realized. As Dallas Willard expertly echoes, "[The] one lesson we learn from all available sources is that there is no 'quick fix' for the human condition. The approach to wholeness is for humankind a process of great length and difficulty that engages all our own powers to their fullest extent over a long course of experience."[1]

How about you?

- Have you ever noticed how restoration, salvation, and recovery are not just destinations but also sometimes experienced like a journey to be patiently endured?
- Have you ever wanted to give up on God's plan because it was going to take longer and cost more than you had planned for?
- Have you ever been under the assumption that submission to God's way would provide deliverance from suffering, consequence, or pain?
- Have you ever noticed your sense of timing differs from God's?

~

Let's get back to Jonah. It is deeply comforting to recognize that Jonah's salvation and deliverance unfold as a gracious process. His journey begins with an initial awareness of his need to stop running and surrender to God. For instance, in chapter 1, we learn that Jonah had already confessed to the sailors that he was fleeing from the Lord. Their incredulous response—"What have you done?"—reflects their understanding of the gravity of his disobedience. This

---

1. Willard, *Spirit*, 5.

Enduring the Process

moment sets the stage for Jonah to begin confronting the reality of his situation.

As the narrative progresses, it becomes evident that both Jonah and the sailors are actively contemplating and connecting the dots. Together, they realize that Jonah needs to stop and turn around. This shared realization paves the way for critical moments in Jonah's process of change, which include his willingness to be thrown overboard, his period of reflection within the belly of the beast, and his ultimate prayerful resolve to obey God. By embracing vulnerability and traveling to Nineveh as commanded, Jonah exemplifies surrender as a dynamic and ongoing process. His deliverance is not achieved through a single act of will but through perseverance and growth, step by step.

In a similar vein, the transtheoretical model of behavioral change illustrates that deliverance and transformation are often a journey rather than a singular event.[2] The model identifies stages such as pre-contemplation, contemplation, and action, while also acknowledging that setbacks, including relapses, are a natural part of the recovery process. Jonah's story mirrors this model, reminding us that surrender is not simply a one-time decision. Instead, it involves an ongoing relational practice of submission and growth. This perspective challenges us to approach our responses to pain with greater intentionality, learning to steward them through vulnerability, persistence, and grace.

Let's specifically examine some stages in Jonah's surrender to God.

First, Jonah's deliverance and surrender appear to be open-ended. We never fully know if Jonah completely surrenders to God. If we had to guess, it might be safer to assume that he does not entirely let go of his hurt. This could be because the story of Jonah resembles many Jewish narratives, in which the ending is left unresolved. Jewish writers often leave stories unfinished to prompt readers to reflect on their own hearts. Thus, the key questions for us are ones of contemplation: *Am I surrendering to God? Am I partnering with God's process of working trust within me?*

2. Prochaska and DiClemente, "Transtheoretical," 38–48.

Drowning in Drama

Second, Jonah experiences a relapse in his surrender to God. In chapter 3, he obeys God's command to proclaim repentance to the Ninevites, but he only does the bare minimum. With that said, Jonah's message is still more than enough; the Ninevites thoroughly repent. And yet, Jonah is left indignant, demonstrating that his inner struggle, or process with hurt and resentment, is far from resolved.

Let's read chapter 4:

> But to Jonah this seemed very wrong, and he became angry. He prayed to the Lord, "Isn't this what I said, Lord, when I was still at home? That is what I tried to forestall by fleeing to Tarshish. I knew that you are a gracious and compassionate God, slow to anger and abounding in love, a God who relents from sending calamity. Now, Lord, take away my life, for it is better for me to die than to live."
>
> But the Lord replied, "Is it right for you to be angry?"
>
> Jonah had gone out and sat down at a place east of the city. There he made himself a shelter, sat in its shade and waited to see what would happen to the city. Then the Lord God provided a leafy plant and made it grow up over Jonah to give shade for his head to ease his discomfort, and Jonah was very happy about the plant. But at dawn the next day God provided a worm, which chewed the plant so that it withered. When the sun rose, God provided a scorching east wind, and the sun blazed on Jonah's head so that he grew faint. He wanted to die, and said, "It would be better for me to die than to live."
>
> But God said to Jonah, "Is it right for you to be angry about the plant?"
>
> "It is," he said. "And I'm so angry I wish I were dead."
>
> But the Lord said, "You have been concerned about this plant, though you did not tend it or make it grow. It sprang up overnight and died overnight. And should I not have concern for the great city of Nineveh, in which there are more than a hundred and twenty thousand people who cannot tell their right hand from their left—and also many animals?"

Enduring the Process

Notice verses 4 and 9. In the former, God asks Jonah, "Is it right for you to be angry?" Jonah refuses to acknowledge God's question, so God asks again later in the chapter, this time using an object lesson for emphasis: "Is it right for you to be angry about the plant?" Here we see Jonah's hard heart explicitly when he says, "It is." Sadly, Jonah seems to have relapsed—perhaps indefinitely—by not partnering with God's process of surrendering his hurt and trust. Instead of choosing vulnerable trust in God, he opts for calloused self-protection.

As I shared earlier in this chapter, the open-ended nature of Jonah's story invites reflection: *Am I surrendering my hurt to God by choosing vulnerability?*

                ∽

For me, this reflection has led to new insights into God's purpose in using processes in our lives. One night in 2005, I was fishing in Cape Cod near Hyannis with a friend when a fishhook was caught in my left eye. I immediately knew this was not good. In fact, when I gently pressed on my eye, I felt aqueous humor—eye fluid—run down my cheek and throat. Somehow, the hook destroyed my lens, causing an instant cataract, but miraculously didn't obliterate my cornea or detach my retina. Praise God! Needless to say, I almost lost my eye and had to patiently endure a long process to both save it and restore my sight.

Over the next year, I underwent multiple surgeries at Yale New Haven Hospital in Connecticut. The doctors knew what needed to be done but couldn't accomplish it all in a single surgery. As they explained to me, my eye, which had already experienced a "large-*T* trauma," would not survive the "small-*t* traumas" of a procedure designed to fix everything at once. In short, the doctors had the knowledge and ability to restore my vision, but my eye couldn't endure such an intrusive rescue all at once. As a result, they developed a step-by-step plan to save my eye, with the hope of eventually restoring my sight. In the end, I received even better eyesight than before, while encountering numerous miracles along the way and a prophetic word that echoes in my ears even now, expressing how I would see things differently than others.

In light of this, I have realized that God graciously submits to processes for our benefit and care—not because he lacks power but because of his love.

ENDURING GOD'S PROCESS OF TRANSFORMATION

1. Will you embrace God's process of surrendering your hurt and trusting Him?

2. Will you patiently and continually submit to the process of vulnerability, or trusting God with your hurt?

3. Which stage of recovery would you place yourself in: pre-contemplation, contemplation, preparation, action, relapse, or maintenance?

Part 2

Sailors

The Rescuers

7

Fear-Driven Responsibility

How Fear and Misplaced Guilt Drive Us to Take On Others' Responsibilities

"[For] God gave us a spirit not of fear but of power and love and self-control."

—2 TIMOTHY 1:7 (ESV)

"Guilt can prevent us from setting the boundaries that would be in our best interests, and in other people's best interests. Guilt can stop us from taking healthy care of ourselves. We don't have to let others count on the fact that we'll always feel guilty. We don't have to allow ourselves to be controlled by guilt—earned or unearned!"

—MELODY BEATTIE, *THE LANGUAGE OF LETTING GO*

IN THIS SECOND PART of the book, we will once again look at the story of Jonah—this time from the perspective of the sailors. As I shared in the introduction, this type of biblical exegesis falls under the interpretation of Scripture known as the tropological sense, offering a map from God that helps morally orient oneself.

Drowning in Drama

By shifting our focus from Jonah to the sailors, we can explore the text from a new angle, revealing insights we may not have previously noticed. This perspective provides a vantage point that draws our attention to the dynamics of not only a Victim but also a Rescuer, or codependent, within a typical drama. It introduces the archetypical Rescuer who can relate to both the dos and don'ts of engaging with a Victim and a Persecutor.

Consequently, I believe there is much we can learn from the sailors. I have personally identified with their rescuing, enabling, and codependent tendencies—patterns that too often encumbered me as I tried to relate to people whom I felt responsible for fixing.

∼

I must admit that, out of the three characters in the Drama Triangle, my default has been the role of the Rescuer. Like the sailors, I have often added to the drama in my relationships by trying to take on the responsibilities of others.

For instance, as I touched on in chapter 5, I wanted to rescue my wife from her feelings of betrayal. But by trying to do so, I interfered with her opportunity to cultivate vulnerability within our community. I complicated and confused the message she felt God was sending her to open up.

Although my wife repeatedly sensed God calling her out of victimhood and into the role of Vulnerable Creator (a role we will explore in the final chapter of this book), I tried to take ownership of her feelings of betrayal—a responsibility that wasn't mine to control or direct. This was impossible: first, because her feelings weren't mine, and second, because I believe what she experienced was indeed a real betrayal. Tragically, my attempt to take responsibility for her feelings kept me from truly empathizing with her.

What I didn't mention earlier is that my fear of her going public—and the perceived sordidness of such an action—motivated me to try to protect the institution from scandal. I felt compelled to take responsibility for *others'* anxiety about her speaking out as well.

Fear-Driven Responsibility

As a result, my wife and other Victims naturally questioned my priorities. Did I care more about addressing the obvious wrongs that I believed God wanted to confront? Or did I care more about the institution and its discomfort with the scandal? More grievous than my fears and questionable priorities was the fact that the person I cared the most about was myself. I cared most about how *I* felt in response to others' thoughts and feelings.

Ultimately, I had to surrender my fear to God and trust that He alone could save both my wife and the people who hurt her. It took me a while to sift through my overwhelming emotions and recognize that my wife shared the same loving concerns. For instance, she had already resolved to act in a way that simultaneously honored God's commands and cared for herself, other Victims, and the institution.

I realized the importance of trusting God with all the people in my life by relinquishing the urge to take responsibility for their emotions and problems. This shift required me to stop attaching to my relationships through anxiety—a pattern that had been deeply ingrained in me. Learning to let go of this anxious attachment allowed me to engage with others more authentically, trusting that God is ultimately in control of their lives and circumstances.

(If this idea of "attaching through anxiety" or having an anxious attachment style resonates with you, I highly recommend exploring attachment theory. It has been an invaluable resource in helping me understand and navigate the dynamics of relationships in a healthier way.[1])

～

Let me give a pop culture example of the Rescuer role, found once again in the movie *Encanto*. (I hope that by now, some of you have watched or re-watched it!) We see this inclination to take on others' responsibilities in the character of Mirabel's sister Luisa.

---

1. For more on attachment theory, see *Attachments: Why You Love, Feel, and Act the Way You Do* by Tim Clinton and Gary Sibcy, and *Anatomy of the Soul: Surprising Connections Between Neuroscience and Spiritual Practices That Can Transform Your Life and Relationships* by Curt Thompson.

Drowning in Drama

Luisa, a muscular young woman, seems able to carry heavy burdens and fix things effortlessly. However, in one scene with Mirabel, Luisa reveals through song that she is not internally at peace when carrying others' burdens, even though she is expected to do so. Luisa admits to her sister that the root of her tendency to be overly responsible for others lies first in the sense of worth she derives from their affirmation. Second, it stems from her fear that if she does not help, everything will fall apart—for both herself and those she loves.

In the song "Surface Pressure," Luisa exposes her fears of what might happen if she stops taking on others' responsibilities. "I'm pretty sure I'm worthless," she says, "if I can't be of service." Her identity is wrapped up in the fact that she carries the burdens for everyone else in the family. The strong sister—it's who she is. This, of course, comes with incredible pressure . . . but no one sees it: "Under the surface, I hide my nerves and it worsens, I worry something is gonna hurt us."[2] On the inside, Luisa is trying hard to hold it all together, not to crack under the pressure.

Luisa's song captures the essence of being guilt-driven. This is the struggle a Rescuer faces when taking on others' responsibilities. For example, she describes a ship that doesn't swerve as it approaches an iceberg, which is much more immense under the surface; in doing so, she lays bare her inner dilemma. On the one hand, she can act to rescue those who are holding her emotionally hostage by playing chicken with the iceberg. On the other hand, she can choose to do nothing and face judgment—not only from those she wants to save but also from her own malformed ego and conscience.

How about you?

- Can you relate to Luisa and other Rescuers?
- Has fear, guilt, or insecurity ever motivated you to feel overly responsible for others?

2. Byron, *Encanto*.

Fear-Driven Responsibility

- Have you ever tended to take on the anxiety, feelings, or problems of others, assuming responsibility for their actions and needs?
- Are you possibly overly anxious when attaching to others?

~

Let's read about the plight of the sailors in Jonah 1:1–16 to see what insights the text offers concerning the role of the Rescuer.

> The word of the LORD came to Jonah son of Amittai: "Go to the great city of Nineveh and preach against it, because its wickedness has come up before me."
>
> But Jonah ran away from the LORD and headed for Tarshish. He went down to Joppa, where he found a ship bound for that port. After paying the fare, he went aboard and sailed for Tarshish to flee from the LORD.
>
> Then the LORD sent a great wind on the sea, and such a violent storm arose that the ship threatened to break up. All the sailors were afraid and each cried out to his own god. And they threw the cargo into the sea to lighten the ship.
>
> But Jonah had gone below deck, where he lay down and fell into a deep sleep. The captain went to him and said, "How can you sleep? Get up and call on your god! Maybe he will take notice of us so that we will not perish."
>
> Then the sailors said to each other, "Come, let us cast lots to find out who is responsible for this calamity." They cast lots and the lot fell on Jonah. So they asked him, "Tell us, who is responsible for making all this trouble for us? What kind of work do you do? Where do you come from? What is your country? From what people are you?"
>
> He answered, "I am a Hebrew and I worship the LORD, the God of heaven, who made the sea and the dry land."
>
> This terrified them and they asked, "What have you done?" (They knew he was running away from the LORD, because he had already told them so.)

> The sea was getting rougher and rougher. So they asked him, "What should we do to you to make the sea calm down for us?"
>
> "Pick me up and throw me into the sea," he replied, "and it will become calm. I know that it is my fault that this great storm has come upon you."
>
> Instead, the men did their best to row back to land. But they could not, for the sea grew even wilder than before. Then they cried out to the Lord, "Please, Lord, do not let us die for taking this man's life. Do not hold us accountable for killing an innocent man, for you, Lord, have done as you pleased." Then they took Jonah and threw him overboard, and the raging sea grew calm. At this the men greatly feared the Lord, and they offered a sacrifice to the Lord and made vows to him.

Did you notice that the sailors already knew Jonah was running from God? In verse 10, we learn that Jonah had told them about his disobedience, yet they become even more terrified as he reveals who his God is and why he is fleeing.

After reading Jonah 1, I have some questions:

- Why would the sailors, knowing that Jonah was running from his God, continue to help him do so?
- Why, despite their growing fear of the precarious situation, would they enable Jonah in his disobedience?
- Why would the sailors work diligently and risk almost everything to save Jonah from the consequences of his disobedient behavior?

Why indeed?

Well, we could first surmise that they are basically good people trying to help, and that's probably a safe assumption. In fact, this is a significant theme in the book of Jonah: God and the author suggest that those who don't know anything about God can be more righteous than God's own people and prophets. However, if we take a fresh look at the text, we also notice that another reason

Fear-Driven Responsibility

is revealed in the sailors' prayer to their gods, disclosing the state of their hearts, which are fearful.

We see throughout the chapter that the sailors have been largely motivated by fear. Specifically, in verse 14, they fear being held responsible by God or their gods if they stop aiding Jonah. I would propose that, like many Rescuers, the sailors' actions and behaviors are driven by a sense of misplaced responsibility. They mistakenly assume responsibility for Jonah's behavior, as illustrated by their sense of guilt for throwing him overboard.

Let's review chapter 1 again, and this time, I'll highlight several instances of misplaced responsibility. In verses 5–6, we see Jonah shirking the natural concerns and responsibilities that a storm like this would normally demand of those on a boat. While the sailors are working hard and praying, Jonah disappears into the lowest part of the ship and tries to escape into a deep sleep. As a result, the frustrated captain challenges Jonah to act more responsibly in this dire situation. In fact, the captain wakes Jonah up with a sharp critique, pointing out that he should already be praying to his god.

Then, in verses 7–10, the storm worsens, leading the sailors to investigate the identity of the guilty party. They cast lots, and the lot falls on Jonah, confirming his culpability. The sailors then confront Jonah, who seems to be holding them hostage by his silence, and they press him with questions, trying to uncover exactly what he has done. This culminates in the storm growing even more violent, and the sailors ask Jonah what they should do to calm it. Jonah finally, though reluctantly, admits his fault and suggests they throw him overboard.

However, Jonah—like a true Victim—refuses to jump into the sea himself. He still avoids taking personal responsibility and declines to act with agency in a disturbance of his own making. Instead, he leaves it up to the sailors, dodging accountability.

In verse 13, we see the sailors continue to take responsibility for Jonah's disobedience. Out of a sense of guilt, they refuse to throw him overboard and instead try to control the ship in the storm. It's only when they reach their limits that it becomes clear they have been owning Jonah's behavior more than he has. They were striving to control not only their situation but even Jonah himself by being overly responsible, assuming responsibility for his feelings, abilities, and behaviors—none of which they had the power to control.

GUILT AND FEAR-DRIVEN RESPONSIBILITY FOR OTHERS

1. Would someone who genuinely loves and cares for you say that you are overly responsible for another loved one?
2. Are you tired and frustrated with a particular relationship? Why?
3. Do you ever feel responsible for another's feelings?
4. Do your behaviors toward a particular person seem to be motivated by guilt or fear-driven responsibility?

8

The Enabling Trap

Even Well-Intentioned Rescuing
May Hinder True Healing

"Put God in charge of your work, then what you have planned will take place."

—Proverbs 16:3 (MSG)

"The simple truth is that loved ones of active addicts are perpetually in crisis mode. Naturally, they try to control the crisis. In the process, they sometimes panic and make bad decisions. They may overdo. They may help too much. They may help ineffectively. They may enable and appear to be pathologically enmeshed. But that does not mean they are psychologically disordered."

—Robert Weiss, *Prodependence*

THERE HAVE BEEN SEVERAL times in my life and ministry when I began to sense that my conscience—an essential critic and guide—was not necessarily aligned with the Father's heart, the Lord's will, or the Spirit's work. On many occasions, while ministering

Drowning in Drama

to people in genuine crisis, I would slip into Rescuer mode, trying to fix or address the obvious needs of others. However, as I've grown in my relationship with God, I've felt moments when he challenged my anxious conscience, telling me: *"Don't touch that. Don't fix that. Don't pray that for them. I know you can resolve that problem, but let's not this time."*

I imagine this may be difficult for some of you to understand, so let me try to explain. Likewise, I sensed in these encounters God reminding me that some problems and people are not mine to fix. God's on it. And I can trust him, especially when the problem or person is not my responsibility. When this is the case in our lives, we may have to walk away, sometimes leaving even the praying up to someone else.[1]

As a default Rescuer, I wrestled with this. The idea of not helping directly challenged the virtues I held—the way I understood what was good or godly. This became a time of personal deconstruction, in which some foundational aspects of my faith were dismantled.

I struggled as God began bringing biblical examples to mind, such as Peter's vision in Acts 10, in which God challenges Peter's and the Church's convictions. God tells Peter to kill and eat food that is unclean according to Jewish law, asking Peter to trust in a God who contradicts his tradition-formed conscience. God seems to go against what he had previously required from his people, yet this shift creates space for the inclusion of the Gentiles, revealing a larger and more complete plan, which God had in mind all along.

I was confronted with other passages, such as Jeremiah 14:11, in which the prophet is told not to pray for God's people. These scriptures acted like outliers, pointing to the possibility that I wasn't always partnering with God's work in others. Instead, I may have been enabling them through misplaced obedience—not obedience to God but rather to my own skewed conscience and conviction.

The author of *Freedom for Obedience* grappled with the ethics of obedience to God when he wrote, "An absolute right sometimes

---

1. For a biblical example, see Jeremiah 7:16-34.

The Enabling Trap

entails relative wrongs. An ethical decision may not be humanly justified, but it may nevertheless be divinely commended."[2]

How about you?

- Have you ever felt that God was asking you *not* to help, even when help was apparently what someone needed?
- Have you ever noticed situations in which your help not only seemed ineffective but even detrimental?

～

This chapter aims to both validate and reevaluate the "virtues" of the Rescuer. It recognizes the hard work, resourcefulness, responsibility, and good intentions that often characterize Rescuers, while also questioning the true helpfulness of these qualities when they're disconnected from a larger, God-centered ideal. The goal is to show how seemingly virtuous actions, if misaligned with God's vision, can actually enable unhealthy dynamics rather than promote genuine healing or change.

Thus, it's insufficient to simply label a Rescuer in the Drama Triangle as an enabler or codependent without first considering the well-intentioned virtues that drive their actions. For instance, Melody Beattie, in *Codependent No More*, notes, "Codependents make great employees. They don't complain; they do more than their share. They do whatever is asked of them; they please people."[3] Similarly, Robert Weiss introduces the concept of "pro-dependents"—caregivers whose intentions are good but whose behaviors and boundaries may lack effectiveness.[4] Through these examples, we can see how the Rescuer's virtues, though admirable, may ultimately fall short without alignment with a more redemptive vision.

---

2. Bloesch, *Freedom*, 59.
3. Beattie, *Codependent*, 52.
4. See *Prodependence: Moving Beyond Codependency* by Robert Weiss.

In light of this, it is important to initially validate the virtues of Rescuers while also acknowledging that they can be misguided without discernment. Likewise, Rescuers often have compassionate, well-meaning intentions that drive their actions. This virtue is so impactful that we'll dedicate an entire later chapter to explore it further. But for now, it's enough to recognize that, like the sailors in Jonah's story, Rescuers in the Drama Triangle may appear virtuous at first glance.

How about you?

- Can you identify with the frustration that comes from the sailors' virtuous hard work, resourcefulness, and responsibility?
- Can you hear from me both an affirmation of your hard work and a challenge to consider that your virtue might not be as virtuous as it seems?
- Could it be possible that your conscience and convictions are not necessarily aligned with God's will in a particular circumstance?
- Can you allow this chapter to push and pull at your foundational beliefs to see if they are truly rooted in Christ and his work in you and others?

~

In summary, a Rescuer's help, motivated by a skewed conscience or guilt, becomes detrimental to everyone involved. In fact, it isn't until the sailors align with God's vision that they shift from enabling to true partnership.

ENDING ENABLEMENT

1. In what ways do the virtues of the Rescuer resonate with you?

The Enabling Trap

2. How have the virtues of the Rescuer malformed the way you relate to others?

3. Can you recall a time when your efforts to help seemed to create more harm?

4. As you reflect on your tendencies to help others, are there areas where you sense God might be inviting you to reevaluate and realign your actions with his will and purpose?

# 9

Good Intentions vs. God's Intent
The Limits of Human Intention

"Jesus answered[,] 'No one is good—except God alone.'"
—MARK 10:18

"It is always with the best intentions that the worst work is done."
—OSCAR WILDE, *MISCELLANEOUS APHORISMS*

"Christ must do a lot of puking when he reflects upon the good works done in his name."
—PAT CONROY, *THE WATER IS WIDE*

AS MENTIONED, I AM a late Gen-Xer, and I wholeheartedly believe some of the best music came out of the nineties. For instance, in 1995, there was a very popular song called "Good Intentions" by Toad the Wet Sprocket. In it, the songwriter wrestles with the idea that one's good intentions do not always lead to the best behaviors or outcomes.

Good Intentions vs. God's Intent

We've all heard someone say, "He or she means well." When this is said, the aftermath of his or her well-meaning scheme was likely less than ideal. Similarly, as a default Rescuer, I have often had good intentions that failed in my actions, and therefore brought about unintended consequences. For example, in previous chapters, I shared about taking responsibility for my wife's feelings of betrayal. In doing so, I tried to rescue her from the pain that I was powerless to address. The problem was that my good intent—wanting to protect her from suffering—actually contributed to her isolation and further suffering. I didn't know then what I know now: that a Victim doesn't have to remain powerless. When they surrender their pain to God, it becomes a wellspring of strength and renewal.

My good intent was limited by my emotional awareness and human understanding. As I related in the earlier chapter, my desire to rescue my wife from her pain conflicted with higher intentions, including God's intent to bring needed justice to a system that tolerated such wrongs.

In the same manner, when we look at the sailors in the book of Jonah, we notice that their actions seem to stem from good intentions. For example, they refuse to throw Jonah overboard at his recommendation. Instead, they row harder, seeking salvation through their own efforts amid the storm.

Let's look at the text of Jonah 1:11–16 (emphasis added), especially the highlighted portion, and notice the framed motive behind the behavior of the sailors:

> The sea was getting rougher and rougher. So they asked him, "What should we do to you to make the sea calm down for us?"
>
> "Pick me up and throw me into the sea," he replied, "and it will become calm. I know that it is my fault that this great storm has come upon you."
>
> Instead, the men did their best to row back to land. But they could not, for the sea grew even wilder than before. *Then they cried out to the Lord, "Please, Lord, do not let us die for taking this man's life. Do not hold us accountable for killing an innocent man, for you, Lord, have*

Drowning in Drama

done as you pleased." Then they took Jonah and threw him overboard, and the raging sea grew calm.

The crew had good intentions! They clearly sought to be dependable sailors who wouldn't lose their cargo, passengers, or ship. This sounds noble. Likewise, in verses 5–10, we see that they want to honor their gods, including the God of Jonah, by being responsive to divine will. Additionally—and most importantly—they do not want to be the cause of Jonah's demise. These behaviors reflect the sailors' underlying good intentions. However, what we ultimately discover in the book of Jonah is that their good intentions fall far short of God's better intent. Their good intentions conflict with God's! In this comparison, their virtue is proven to be a façade.

∼

For me, and I suspect for many of you as well, this is confounding—a seeming paradox. How can good intentions be detrimental? How can bad come from good intent? How does evil find a place within one's good intentions?

The answers seem to lie in the sailors' ignorance of the information needed to inform their good intent and, subsequently, in their capacity to attend to God, the source of ultimate good. I may have just lost some of you here, so let's take some time to unpack this.

There can be multiple—maybe even limitless—good intentions because good intent is somewhat subjective to an individual's perception. The questions, then, are as follows: If there are limitless possible good intentions, are some better than others? And what would make some good intentions better? Subsequently, is there an apex of *good*? Well, the greatest good intention would presumably involve all the facts necessary to inform what would be the greatest good. In light of this, the apex of good is naturally an omniscient God, who is not ignorant of anything and thus has the most information for forming the best intent for what is good for all.

Let's say the sailors know what will happen—they know that God has prepared a massive sea creature beneath the surface to save Jonah. They would probably conclude that God's intent is

Good Intentions vs. God's Intent

better than they first presumed. The obvious problem is that a sea creature, acting both as a submarine for Jonah and a womb for his heart transformation, is not in the realm of their foreseeable solutions. Trusting God to do beyond what we can imagine is hard!

In other words, their ignorance causes their good intent to be far less good than God's perfectly informed intent. The sailors' good intentions toward Jonah, themselves, and even God are limited by their ignorance—limited to their understanding of what is truly good and what is happening within the larger context of both the Ninevites' need for repentance and Jonah's own hard heart.

Additionally, if God is the source of the greatest good because he has the most information available to inform what is good, then those who look to him as the source of their intent have the capacity for this goodness to fill them and flow through them. Therefore, it is not enough for a Rescuer to have merely good intentions; they must have God as the source of their intent.

I would even argue that the sailors' good intentions to save Jonah and others are not truly good. Why? Because they aren't good enough! Their intentions fall woefully short of trusting God to save. Furthermore, their efforts do not address the fundamental issues: the Ninevites' need to repent and be saved and Jonah's hardened heart, which is resistant to allowing God to address his history of hurt. It is only when the sailors' behaviors align with God's intent that the best, most complete good is realized.

∼

Considering this, we can understand evil's continued existence as a repercussion of free-willed behaviors by beings who do not fully look to God as their source for discerning good. Pseudo-Dionysius, a medieval writer who introduced negative theology, suggests this in his remarkable work *The Names of God*. For Dionysius, evil flourishes in the sphere of those not attending to God's vision or intent—the greatest good. For Dionysius, true "Good" is essentially another name for God.[1]

---

1. Luibheid, *Pseudo-Dionysius*, 71–96.

Drowning in Drama

Similarly, the late French philosopher Albert Camus articulates this idea well when he says, "The evil that is in this world always comes of ignorance, and good intentions may do as much harm as malevolence, if they lack understanding."[2]

Practically speaking, much evil can arise from ignorance—from the gap between a Rescuer's good intentions and God's intent. A popular example of evil resulting from good intentions can be found in the acclaimed television series *Breaking Bad*. Walter White, the main character, begins with good intentions. Recently diagnosed with terminal cancer, White wants to provide for his family. As a chemistry teacher without any savings, he sees an opportunity in cooking and selling meth to secure a nest egg for the family he will soon leave behind.

Sadly, as the series unfolds, White's actions produce all kinds of evil, despite his well-meaning. His understanding of goodness is repeatedly shown to be too limited. His "good" is governed by his inability to know everything, including what will happen in the future. As a result, his good intent falls far short of a more complete and perfect good. Spoiler alert: Bad is not broken!

How about you?

- Can you relate to the Rescuer and sailors who had subjectively good intentions?
- Do your intentions flow from the source of God and his intent?

∼

Why do we so often choose our good intentions over God's intent? If you're like me, there's something more inviting and comforting about my intentions. My intentions are within the realm of my conscious control, and that knowing provides a false, yet real, comfort. It gives me an excuse to be a responsible—if perhaps enabling—Rescuer.

---

2. Camus, *The Plague*, 126.

Good Intentions vs. God's Intent

In contrast, God's intent is more mysterious and resides in the omniscience of God himself. It requires faith and trust. It requires me to surrender control—not an easy task for a Rescuer like me.

GOOD INTENTIONS OR GOD'S INTENT?

1. Would others close to you describe your good intentions as being God's intent for you and others?
2. Do you ever let God and Scripture evaluate what you have deemed as a good intention?
3. Do your behaviors align with God's intent—with his vision for that relationship or situation?

10

Surrendering Control

The Freedom and Peace of Trusting God's Greater Plan over Our Own Desired Outcomes

"Trust in the Lord with all your heart; do not depend on your own understanding. Seek his will in all you do, and he will show you which path to take."
—Proverbs 3:5–6 (NLT)

"Sometimes we have to give up the values we cherish in order to follow Christ into darkness."
—Donald G. Bloesch, *Freedom for Obedience*

"You are afraid to surrender because you do not want to lose control. But you never had control; all you had was anxiety."
—(attributed to) Elizabeth Gilbert

One of my first memories as a young boy is of waking up in the middle of the night to a loud disruption and hearing my mom yelling my dad's name. I remember running into my parents' room

Surrendering Control

to find my dad violently shaking on the floor. My mom, a nurse, was huddled over him, looking into his mouth, holding his head, and screaming his name.

At some point in my maturity, I filled in this memory with adult details: my dad was having a seizure, and my mom was trying to keep him from biting his tongue. If you've ever witnessed someone suffering a grand mal seizure, you know it's truly terrifying—especially for a three- or four-year-old boy.

During this traumatic episode, I remember my mom looking over at me and asking me to call for help. That help would have been my grandmother, but I was too young—or too shocked—to remember her number. I stood there stunned, frozen, afraid, and powerless to help, though I desperately wanted to. My mom eventually ran into the living room and called for help. In the end, the paramedics came, and everything turned out fine... except for me.

That moment became a traumatic experience—one that emphasized the real dangers in our world and, most significantly, my powerlessness in scary situations. Somehow, in that time and place, I unconsciously made an inner vow: I would never be powerless to help those I loved again. I would be prepared and ready. I would be enough for any situation. I would fight and not stand stunned. Later in life, when confronted with fearful experiences, I would unconsciously strive for control and even use anger as a nuclear option to regain an elusive sense of security.

Control is such an elusive illusion! We have just enough of it to feel like we can steer our situation, but never enough to stop ourselves from being disoriented by the chaos around us. Ultimately, our desire for control is an overattachment to a good intention.

Psychologist Julian Rotter introduced a personality theory called the locus of control, which suggests that people believe they have varying degrees of control over situations and outcomes.[1] In light of this theory, a Rescuer's personality tends to assume they have more power over situations—and therefore outcomes—than

---

1. See "Generalized Expectancies for Internal Versus External Control of Reinforcement" by Julian B. Rotter in *Psychological Monographs: General and Applied*.

they really do. This illusion leads to anxiety, fear, control, anger, and ultimately disillusionment.

Fortunately, it also leads to the necessary surrender of our good intentions and desired outcomes to a powerful and omniscient God.

How about you?

- Have you experienced the illusion of control over things and people, only to later realize it was elusive?
- Have you ever realized that your being in control often looks like you're not exercising self-control?
- Have you ever been overly attached to a desired outcome or good intention?

~

Let's look at Jonah 1:11–16 (emphasis added) and learn once again from the sailors:

> The sea was getting rougher and rougher. So they asked him, "What should we do to you to make the sea calm down for us?"
> "Pick me up and throw me into the sea," he replied, "and it will become calm. I know that it is my fault that this great storm has come upon you."
> *Instead, the men did their best to row back to land. But they could not, for the sea grew even wilder than before.* Then they cried out to the LORD, "Please, LORD, do not let us die for taking this man's life. Do not hold us accountable for killing an innocent man, for you, LORD, have done as you pleased." Then they took Jonah and threw him overboard, and the raging sea grew calm. At this the men greatly feared the LORD, and they offered a sacrifice to the LORD and made vows to him.

Notice how the sailors' attempts to achieve their desired outcome only lead to more chaos? Their efforts to control the

Surrendering Control

situation become an exercise in grasping and forcing their environment, resulting in an uproar rather than a resolution. In fact, one could argue that their attempts at control only fuel the chaotic circumstances they face. Despite their repeated efforts to make the ship more maneuverable, they find the storm increasingly difficult to navigate. It's as if they are artists trying to sculpt with a material that is too liquid or pliable to hold any desired shape.

Ultimately, the sailors come to the crucial realization that the only thing they can truly control is their ability to surrender. This means they must not only let go of Jonah, their dependent, but also release their attachment to their own desired outcome of being responsible. They need to trust in God's desired outcome over their own plans.

In verses 14–15, we see the sailors connect their act of throwing Jonah overboard with their surrender, calling out to Yahweh, the God of Jonah. As they prepare to act, they plead, "Do not let us die for taking this man's life. Do not hold us accountable for killing an innocent man, for you, LORD, have done as you pleased." This reveals their understanding that they are acting in accordance with God's will, even as they face the reality that throwing Jonah overboard is in all likelihood a death sentence.

Remarkably, what appears to be an act of desperation is in truth a profound demonstration of the sailors' trust in God to save. They acknowledge the gravity of their decision while trusting that God may still intervene. In this way, the sailors' surrender mirrors the peace experienced by Rescuers who choose to surrender their dependents to God. This profound trust becomes a pathway to peace, transforming chaos into hope.

∼

I'm reminded of yet another Disney movie with parallels to Jonah. *Finding Nemo* is a story about an overprotective fish named Marlin, the quintessential Rescuer, who is trying to find his missing son. In one suspenseful, yet comic scene, Marlin and his seemingly mindless companion Dory have been swallowed by a whale. They are stuck in the whale's mouth when Dory, who claims to "speak whale," tells Marlin that the whale says they need to go to the back of its throat.

Marlin is holding on for dear life and berating Dory for ridiculously claiming to speak whale *and* for believing the whale when it speaks.

"Of course, he wants us to go there! That's eating us," Marlin exclaims. "You tell him I'm not interested in being lunch."

When the whale "speaks" again, Dory interprets: "He says it's time to *let go*. Everything is going to be all right."

"How do you know something bad isn't going to happen?" Marlin pleads.

Dory admits that she doesn't know. But the two fish let go and are ultimately expelled through the whale's blowhole and go on to be reunited with Marlin's son, Nemo.[2]

This scene serves as a fitting metaphor for the tension those of us Rescuers feel. We can understand Marlin's protests. If he's eaten by the whale, then he can't rescue his son. He can't just let go! But his semblance of control in this scenario is pointless. Whereas Dory meekly surrenders her vulnerability to the whale. She trusts it because she speaks its language. And her trust pays off because the whale takes them to where Nemo is.

We, like Marlin, don't have all the information. We don't speak whale. Besides that, it's a vast ocean, and we can't see all of it with our limited perspective. But whether we're in the mouth of the whale or the belly of a great fish, we don't have many options.

How do we know nothing bad is going to happen when we surrender? We don't. But if we let go, the inner chaos will stop, and we just might save not only ourselves but also those we love.

∽

Yes, true peace is the result of a Rescuer surrendering their desired outcome to God's better outcome. As we see in the story of Jonah, the storm immediately stops, signaling the alignment of Jonah and

---

2. Stanton, *Finding Nemo*.

Surrendering Control

the sailors with God's will in the cosmos. This is real peace for the sailors—a peace that literally saves them.

However, as I mentioned in earlier chapters, this doesn't mean that things get immediately better. In fact, as we see, things get worse, particularly for Jonah. And things may not be perfect for the sailors either. They may never know what happens to Jonah. All they might know is the peace from the storm that comes after giving Jonah what seems to be a death sentence. Can you imagine their questions and feelings of personal guilt?

For the sailors, surrendering control provides God the opportunity to rescue those in need around them, including Jonah. This is clearly demonstrated when God provides the sea creature beneath the surface of the storm-tossed sea. The creature is ready to eat—uh, I mean, *save* Jonah, in more ways than one!

Please understand this: Surrendering the urge to save those we love is often a painful and scary experience. It can feel like abandoning our loved ones to chaos and certain death. It may even feel like we are feeding them to sea monsters. However, the rescue that God accomplishes in our surrender looks more like death *and* resurrection. What I mean by this is that parts of both the Rescuer and the Victim have to die as a sacrifice through surrender to God.

In this same vein, Oswald Chambers states, "True surrender will always go beyond natural devotion. If we will only give up, God will surrender Himself to embrace all those around us and will meet their needs, which were created by our surrender. Beware of stopping anywhere short of total surrender to God."[3]

I want to take a moment to riff on Chambers's idea here. The Rescuer's surrender of good intentions and control to God brings the Victim's needs into clearer focus. In doing so, the Victim can plainly see their greater need for God. Likewise, the Rescuer steps into the role of a Caring Coach, who first models surrender to God and then points the Victim toward their ultimate need to embrace vulnerability. Subsequently, God surrenders himself to the needs of the Victim, extending an invitation for the Victim to offer their vulnerability to him.

3. Chambers, *My Utmost*, July 13.

Drowning in Drama

The Rescuer's act of surrender often resembles the sailors throwing Jonah overboard into a storm. This surrender may feel scandalously wrong. It probably even feels like a denial of self, good, and even God. However, it is a resting in God—a trust that he remains true to his character. Richard Foster says in his monumental book *The Celebration of Discipline*, "[Self-denial] means the freedom to give way to others [including God]. It means to hold others' interests above self-interest. In this way self-denial releases from self-pity."[4]

"Self-denial" for the Rescuer is an act of faith in God to save themselves and those they love. It frees them from striving to earn their own righteousness and defining their significance by their responsibilities. Additionally, the Rescuer's self-denial holds a hopeful possibility for the salvation of loved ones through surrender to God.

SURRENDERING CONTROL

1. How do you find yourself relating to the sailors?
2. Can you identify a time when you felt God was asking you to release someone you loved to his care, even though it felt like abandoning them to chaos and uncertainty?
3. What fears and doubts arise in you when you think about giving those you feel responsible for to God?

---

4. Foster, *Celebration*, 113–14.

11

Misplaced Sympathy

How Misplaced Sympathies Hinder God's Work

"Do not suppose that I have come to bring peace to the earth. I did not come to bring peace, but a sword. For . . . 'a man's enemies will be the members of his own household.' Anyone who loves their father or mother more than me is not worthy of me. Whoever does not take up their cross and follow me is not worthy of me. Whoever finds their life will lose it, and whoever loses their life for my sake will find it."

—Matthew 10:34–39

"Never be sympathetic with a person whose situation causes you to conclude that God is dealing harshly with him. God can be more tender than we can conceive, and every once in a while He gives us the opportunity to deal firmly with someone so that He may be viewed as the tender One."

—Oswald Chambers, *My Utmost for His Highest*

As I shared earlier, I, the default Rescuer, took undue responsibility for the fallout of my wife's public disclosure. I was anxiously attached to how my peers and respected leaders would react. This attachment of mine hurt my wife and other Victims—a regrettable form of complicity on my part.

What I am trying to say is that my sympathy was misplaced. It was focused on me and my feelings. This misplaced sympathy skewed my sense of justice. Thankfully, God would not tolerate this in me. Instead, he lovingly challenged and faithfully corrected my self-pity.

First, he sent clear signs that he was weighing in on the conversation. Like the storm in the book of Jonah, like the cast lot that fell to Jonah, God communicated that he was symbolically engaging in the situation, showing us that he had something to say about these wrongs. Second, I sensed God critiquing my misplaced sympathies and urging me to take a firm, even harsh, stance against injustices that he would no longer tolerate. As it was not up to me to save anyone from their feelings, it was also not up to me to save anyone from their reckoning.

How about you?

- Can you relate to having misplaced your sympathies?
- Have you ever prioritized the wrong feelings, people, or things?
- Have you ever left a difficult conversation feeling that you weren't as firm—and therefore as lovingly caring—as you should have been?

∽

Let's take one more look at the sailors in Jonah 1:11–16 (emphasis added):

> "Pick me up and throw me into the sea," he replied, "and it will become calm. I know that it is my fault that this great storm has come upon you."
> *Instead*, the men did their best to row back to land. But they could not, for the sea grew even wilder than

Misplaced Sympathy

before. *Then they cried out to the* LORD, "Please, LORD, do not let us die for taking this man's life. Do not hold us accountable for killing an innocent man, for you, LORD, have done as you pleased." Then they took Jonah and threw him overboard, and the raging sea grew calm. At this the men greatly feared the LORD, and they offered a sacrifice to the LORD and made vows to him.

In this passage, we see a significant weakness in the sailors: they refuse to be strong in support of God's stance. Their concerns are more focused on themselves and Jonah rather than on God, the Ninevites, and even the Israelites. Their sympathies are simply misplaced.

They won't stand firm on what God reveals needs to be done. Why? Because, as I have shared in an earlier chapter, they over-identify with their good intentions and desired outcomes. Furthermore, they see themselves as more powerful than they actually are while simultaneously viewing Jonah as less powerful than he truly is.

In short, their over-identification with good intentions has led to insecurity and, consequently, a willingness to compromise their compassion. Their sympathies are misplaced, as they pity their difficult situation instead of focusing on Jonah's hardened heart and the broader needs of both the Ninevites and Israelites. The sailors' concern is more for themselves and about being perceived as irresponsible and harsh. Similarly, Rescuers are generally unaware that their efforts to control a narrative that frames them in a good light can be rather selfish.

How truly unloving! Consider what Dietrich Bonhoeffer wrote: "Nothing can be more cruel than the leniency which abandons others to their sin. Nothing can be more compassionate than the severe rebuke which calls another Christian in one's community back from the path of sin."[1]

Eventually, however, the sailors cut Jonah loose and, by so doing, hand him a death sentence. And yet, this harsh act is mysteriously loving, providing a miraculous opportunity for God to

---

1. Bonhoeffer, *Life*, 107.

act. The sailors' surrender secures them in the trust of God's will. In this final act of righteous obedience, they are tough yet also loving when seen in the larger context of how their surrender affects everyone. They love much by allowing God to love all involved. It's fascinating that the sailors' display of faith in God through surrender becomes the gateway to numerous other miracles, such as the Ninevites' repentance and salvation.

A common example of the Drama and Winner's Triangles can be found in a familiar trope from TV and movies about police: the "Good Cop, Bad Cop" dynamic during an interrogation. In these dramas, one officer assumes the role of the Good Cop, while the other plays the Bad Cop. This relational setup aims to reveal the objective truth hidden within subjective perceptions. Here, the Bad Cop isn't necessarily "bad" but serves rather to challenge the current relational status quo. Predictably, the suspect being interrogated gravitates toward the Good Cop—or the Rescuer in the Drama Triangle—seeking sympathy and saving. However, in the Winner's Triangle, the Good Cop does not step in to rescue but instead coaches the one under interrogation, encouraging them to share the truth with honesty and vulnerability.

This example also provides a model for how God invites the Rescuer to save by surrendering control. As Oswald Chambers suggests in the excerpt quoted at the beginning of this chapter, there are times when we are called to take on a challenging role, guiding others to surrender to God by lovingly refraining from taking charge.[2] This approach helps reveal the deeper need for our surrender to God's love and truth.

Stanley Hauerwas writes, "The credibility of Christians is hurt not by their failure of good will, but their refusal to face the reality that even good will cannot act without hurting. The greatest enemy of the Christian life is not self-interest, but sentimentality."[3]

2. Chambers, *My Utmost*, December 19.
3. Hauerwas, *Vision*, 119.

Misplaced Sympathy

Imagine with me the possibilities that God has for us beneath the surface of our drama if we would only rightly place our sympathies to include God, others, and ourselves, and not just the Victim. Imagine what God could do in the lives of those we love if we took a firm, and sometimes necessarily harsh, stance toward those who need to stop running from him.

FIRM AND PRIORITIZED SYMPATHIES

1. Would you be willing to consider that your self-pity may be a cloaked form of narcissism?
2. Are you more sympathetic toward yourself than others?
3. Do you ever get in the way of God's salvation for others?
4. Do your behaviors reveal misplaced sympathies?

Part 3

Ninevites
The Persecutors

12

Blinded by Greatness

The Allure of Greatness Obscures Moral Clarity

"Samuel saw Eliab and thought, 'Surely the Lord's anointed stands here before the Lord.' But the Lord said to Samuel, 'Do not consider his appearance or his height....'"

—1 Samuel 16:6–7

"Do not expect justice where might equals right."

—Plato, *The Republic*

"Success is not the name of God."

—Dietrich Bonhoeffer

In this third part of the book, we will focus on the Persecutor through the prescriptive example of the Ninevites. I imagine most readers, when reflecting on the role of the Persecutor, are hesitant to consider that they may have, at times, fulfilled this part. After all, who wants to think of themselves as a bully or even a tyrant? Not I!

Drowning in Drama

However, driven by my own agenda and often at the expense of those around me, I have all too often misused my power to coerce and intimidate others. It has only been through God's grace, illustrated in the lessons of the Ninevites, that I've recognized my need for humility. My hope is that you might also consider the possibility that you have, on occasion, played the part of the Persecutor—and that you might learn from the Ninevites' example of surrender.

Ultimately, the goal of this third part of the book is to present God's invitation to those in the role of the Persecutor to surrender their power to God and align with his vision. My desire is for the Persecutor to exit the Drama Triangle and enter the Winner's Triangle by surrendering their power to God.

~

Let's look at *Star Wars* again as an example of the dynamics in the Drama Triangle. (My apologies if you do not share my enthusiasm for the franchise!)

Throughout the prequel trilogy, Anakin transitions into the iconic villain, Darth Vader. He even takes on a new name as he steps into the role of Persecutor. What's fascinating about Anakin, though, is that there are two sides to him. First, there's something undeniably *special* about him. He has unique gifts and a sense of purpose that set him apart—he's the "chosen one,"[1] as Obi-Wan says. But he's also a real villain, and his "dark side" tragically overshadows his greatness.

Even so, I'd suggest that his villainy doesn't fully erase Anakin's greatness. Despite being polluted, his greatness is still part of who he is. It surfaces once again in *Return of the Jedi* when he, as Darth Vader, chooses to save his son from the Emperor, which redeems him in a powerful way.

When watching *Star Wars*, I have mixed reactions to Vader. I catch myself appreciating certain aspects of his character while also feeling repulsed. It's strange because, on the one hand, his

---

1. Lucas, *Episode 3*.

Blinded by Greatness

greatness is so evident; yet on the other, he uses it for selfish ambition without regard for others. He even goes as far as murdering younglings—the children being trained in the Jedi Order—which is *greatly* evil.

Of course, I don't admire his selfishness or his disregard for others, especially the vulnerable, such as younglings. But over time, I've come to better understand my conflicting feelings about Vader. While I don't admire his cruelty, I do recognize his raw ability, ambition, authority, and power.

I admire Vader's greatness.

Likewise, in my personal life, I can attest to how difficult it is to reconcile the greatness of my Persecutors with the harm they caused.

Yes, I am admitting that those who have played the part of Persecutor in my life had admirable, applaudable qualities that should be acknowledged. But hear me out: My admiration for their greatness made it hard to resolve their standing when considering their wrongs. Their abilities were impressive, yet their purposes for using those abilities were weak and, I believe, missed the heart of God.

These conflicting messages created an illusion for me. My Persecutors' brilliance acted as a blinding light, leading to a disillusionment that needed to be dismantled, addressed, and discerned. Notably, this was not solely their fault but also partly mine. I, along with most others, shared the same blindness as my Persecutors by participating in the joint illusion that greatness somehow grants permission. I unconsciously took greatness's potential as a moral validation of behavior.

This is an increasingly prevalent dynamic in our pragmatic world today. For instance, our society is bombarded with new innovations and technologies. In science, we pursue opportunities and possibilities without fully considering the moral ramifications of these advancements. In short, the greatness of technology often blinds us to the future detrimental effects of these advances and the subsequent pathologies they create.

In light of this, I can also personally relate to the illusion that greatness somehow grants license! When I have been in the role

Drowning in Drama

of the Persecutor, I've had great abilities that provided me with possibilities others admired. This meant that I had not only merit but also an enormous responsibility to God for those who were vulnerable to my influence and power.

While I was often consciously aware that my abilities required responsibility, I also unconsciously used my greatness as a stamp of validation, as if God were endorsing my personal ambitions and resulting behaviors. In each of these situations, it became apparent that God was not always validating my behaviors but rather exercising patience and mercy toward me. In short, while my greatness granted possibility, these same possibilities did not always equate to God's permission.

Persecutors, Victims, and Rescuers often unconsciously perceive ability as permission. They tacitly frame greatness as a grant of consent. Or, put another way, no matter what role we find ourselves playing, we may allow the power available to us to qualify as a right. In short, this chapter explores the idea that Victims, Rescuers, and especially Persecutors too often become blinded by greatness, assuming it constitutes moral authority and permission for one's personal prerogatives. However, a distinction must be made to see clearly and deconstruct the illusion that greatness grants permission.

How about you?

- Have you ever unconsciously used your ability or greatness as moral validation for your behavior?
- Have you ever assumed that the possibilities afforded by greatness granted you permission?
- Have you ever concluded that just because you can, of course, you should?

Blinded by Greatness

Let's reflect on this more deeply by exploring what the story of Jonah reveals about a Persecutor's greatness. The obvious thing about the Ninevites and the Assyrian Empire is that they were, indeed, great. They possessed a utility and worth that were admirable and fearful to all. When I mention *greatness*, I imagine you, like me, may initially think it a primary category of moral goodness. However, it's important to clarify that the Ninevites were not *morally* great. Obviously, that's not what God means when he refers to Nineveh as a great city.

For example, in chapters 1, 3, and 4 of Jonah, God describes Nineveh as a "great city." He instructs Jonah to go to the "great city of Nineveh" and preach against the Ninevites because he has heard of their wickedness. Clearly, God is referring to Nineveh's greatness as something other than moral goodness, or he wouldn't be sending Jonah to confront its wickedness. In short, God is separating Nineveh's greatness from its morality. God is inviting the Ninevites to surrender their greatness to his vision for both them and the world.

This raises the question: If Nineveh's greatness is not a measure of morality, then what is it?

Let's look at the third chapter of Jonah to see if, once again, this book offers answers:

> Then the word of the LORD came to Jonah a second time: "Go to the great city of Nineveh and proclaim to it the message I give you."
>
> Jonah obeyed the word of the LORD and went to Nineveh. Now Nineveh was a very large city; it took three days to go through it. Jonah began by going a day's journey into the city, proclaiming, "Forty more days and Nineveh will be overthrown." The Ninevites believed God. A fast was proclaimed, and all of them, from the greatest to the least, put on sackcloth.
>
> When Jonah's warning reached the king of Nineveh, he rose from his throne, took off his royal robes, covered himself with sackcloth and sat down in the dust. This is the proclamation he issued in Nineveh:
>
> "By the decree of the king and his nobles:

Drowning in Drama

"Do not let people or animals, herds or flocks, taste anything; do not let them eat or drink. But let people and animals be covered with sackcloth. Let everyone call urgently on God. Let them give up their evil ways and their violence. Who knows? God may yet relent and with compassion turn from his fierce anger so that we will not perish."

When God saw what they did and how they turned from their evil ways, he relented and did not bring on them the destruction he had threatened."

Nineveh's greatness is evident in its vast size, sophisticated capabilities, and unique role in God's plan. First, Nineveh's greatness is marked by its sheer size and, consequently, its power. As a large city with abundant resources and a substantial population, it holds significant influence. In Jonah 3:3, Nineveh is described as "a very large city," underscoring its impressive scale. This is further emphasized by the fact that it takes three days to traverse the city.

Interestingly, the Ninevites begin to repent after Jonah has traveled only a day's journey within it. Later, in chapter 4, the author highlights Nineveh's population as exceeding 120,000 people, with a multitude of animals as well. This emphasis on size and resources underscores the first marker of Nineveh's greatness—its scale and the power that accompanies it.

The second notable aspect of Nineveh's greatness is its enormous capabilities. It was indeed a highly sophisticated empire. Nineveh was part of the Neo-Assyrian Empire, and according to various archaeological accounts and commentaries, it had a standing army, a library, a network of roads and laws, and administrative prowess unmatched by any other civilization of the time.[2]

Here's a brief overview of the Assyrian Empire. It appears to be one of several derivatives of an earlier Bronze Age Mesopotamian empire that had collapsed.[3] Assyria, as the last man standing after the fall of the initial Mesopotamian empire, eventually dominated the Levant and the kingdoms of Urartu, Aram, and Israel. As

---

2. See *Assyria: The Rise and Fall of the World's First Empire* by Eckart Frahm.

3. Grayson, "Assyria and Babylonia," 140–94.

Blinded by Greatness

prophesied in the book of Nahum, the Assyrian Empire eventually fell to the Neo-Babylonian Empire in the Iron Age.

This history is corroborated in Scripture. For instance, the founding peoples of Assyria and Nineveh are documented as great and powerful, and they used this power and greatness to dominate others.[4] The Assyrian Empire traces back to the builders of the Tower of Babel, with their archetypal leader Nimrod, whose name means "rebellion," described as a "mighty hunter."[5]

Interestingly, many Bible commentators suggest that Nimrod's title describes someone who hunted humans and neighboring city-states; this definition defies God's vision for humanity not to dominate one another.[6] In other words, the label "mighty hunter" depicts Nimrod, Babylon, and the Assyrian Empire as ambitious empire-builders rather than big-game hunters. These commentators interpret Genesis 10 to mean that Nimrod's people used violence and threats of violence to dominate others.

Let's look at the text of Genesis 10:8–12:

> Cush was the father of Nimrod, who became a mighty warrior on the earth. He was a mighty hunter before the Lord; that is why it is said, "Like Nimrod, a mighty hunter before the Lord." The first centers of his kingdom were Babylon, Uruk, Akkad and Kalneh, in Shinar. From that land he went to Assyria, where he built Nineveh, Rehoboth Ir, Calah and Resen, which is between Nineveh and Calah—which is the great city.

Additionally, the book of Jonah corroborates Nineveh's sophistication. For instance, not only the king but also the entire populace of the city repents—and they do so quickly and thoroughly. This is a clear sign of Nineveh's readiness and virtue, in contrast to Israel's unresponsiveness to God. However, it also offers a glimpse into Nineveh's well-developed systems of communication and implementation.

---

4. Cook, "Blessed," 363–68.
5. van der Kooij, "Babel," 1–17.
6. Hom, "Mighty," 63–68.

This sophistication even extends to the Assyrians' control over resources, as demonstrated by the decree in Jonah 3:8 that even animals should show signs of repentance. Interestingly, the Assyrian Empire's logistical prowess, combined with knowledge and skill, enabled it to project power across multiple areas of culture, including regional politics, technology, religion, and commerce.[7] Its sophistication made the empire an unparalleled logistical and technological power for its time.

The third, often unconsidered yet significant, reason God refers to Nineveh as "great" is that he sees a unique, purposeful utility in it. Uri Brito and Rich Lusk state in their commentary on Jonah, *The Reluctant Prophet*, "The city was great in God's eyes because God was planning to use Nineveh for his own purposes. In a sense, Nineveh becomes God's chosen city."[8] Thus, Nineveh is a city chosen by God to help restrain, retrain, or discipline other nations, including his rebellious, *chosen* people of Israel.

This can be confounding! Such an idea about an enemy challenges our natural biases. How can God justly see a potential partnership in Nineveh's ability, size, and position for his purposes in the world, given their pride, immorality, wickedness, and violence?

Yet, as Thomas Aquinas said, "God himself would not permit evil in this world if good did not come of it for the benefit and harmony of the universe."[9]

How about you?

- Are you at all blinded by greatness?
- Can you, like me—and like the Ninevites—admit to unconsciously acting under the assumption that greatness not only grants possibilities but also permissions?

---

7. See *Assyria: The Rise and Fall of the World's First Empire* by Eckart Frahm.

8. Brito and Lusk, *The Reluctant Prophet*, 37.

9. Knight, *Summa Theologiae*. "Prima Pars," Q. 49.

Blinded by Greatness

- Have you ever done something simply because you could, only to have God later challenge your actions and invite you to align your greatness and power with his vision?

∼

At this point, I think it's important to unpack this suggestion to avoid misunderstanding. I am not saying that God condones Nineveh's wrongful behaviors. This is clearly not the case, as God sends Jonah to judge and warn the Ninevites of their impending destruction because of their wickedness.

Furthermore, I am not suggesting that a Victim's detrimental experience at the hands of a Persecutor is God's will. For example, later on in history, Nineveh does not honor God's vision for its greatness, and Israel suffers many tragedies at the hands of the Assyrians that God did not wish or permit. Because of this, God justly judges Nineveh, condemning its people for using their greatness and power for their own vision rather than his. They misuse their power, exceeding God's will, and are ultimately punished for it.

What then am I trying to say? I am proposing that God can justly and patiently invite Persecutors into his plans, utilizing their greatness while simultaneously holding them accountable for any wrongs or abuses of that greatness along the way. Interestingly, the prophet Isaiah speaks to this very idea in Isaiah 10:5–7:

> Woe to the Assyrian, the rod of my anger, in whose hand is the club of my wrath! I send him against a godless nation, I dispatch him against a people who anger me, to seize loot and snatch plunder, and to trample them down like mud in the streets. But this is not what he intends, this is not what he has in mind; his purpose is to destroy, to put an end to many nations.

Isaiah describes Assyria as a tool for God's purpose of purifying hypocritical nations. Yet he also suggests that God knows the Assyrians' intentions and will hold them accountable for exceeding the scope of power he intended.

Drowning in Drama

In light of this complex interplay, I think it's essential to see ourselves as embodying each role in the Drama Triangle at different times. Each of us has a default pattern, which may lead us to be the Persecutor in our own dramas. Subsequently, it's helpful to recognize when we have stepped into the Persecutor's role and humbly consider that God often delays judgment. Only by doing so can we begin to grasp why God patiently allows and ultimately uses Persecutors in his purposes. If God excluded Persecutors entirely, we would all at some point find ourselves excluded.

I personally thank God for his loving patience and grace, as there have been times when I have quickly shifted from my default role as Rescuer to Victim and then to Persecutor. As a Persecutor, I've needed God to patiently guide me back to his vision before being harshly judged or exposed before others. I often need the reminder, as in Jonah 4:11, that the Ninevites did not know their right from their left. Similarly, Persecutors like myself can be blinded by a sense of greatness and need God's gentle process of clarity, or else they may face severe judgment.

Now that I've clarified what I mean by God partnering with Persecutors to align them with his plans, I want to return to and restate the main point of this chapter: Victims, Rescuers, and especially Persecutors can often be deceived and blinded by greatness.

MIGHT DOES NOT EQUAL RIGHT

1. Have you ever unconsciously used your talents, abilities, or influences to validate your behavior? How did you come to realize this?
2. Have you ever admired someone for their greatness, only to feel conflicted when their actions didn't align with moral or godly principles?
3. Can you identify an area in your own life where you have been blinded by greatness?

13

The Persecutor's Privilege

The Responsibility of People in Power

"Masters, provide your slaves with what is right and fair, because you know that you also have a Master in heaven."

—Colossians 4:1

"The greater the power, the more dangerous the abuse."

—Edmund Burke

"God does not give people status and privilege for their own sake but in order that through them he may bless the world."

—N. T. Wright, *Paul and the Faithfulness of God*

In recent years, numerous movies and shows have explored the problem of power differentials gone wrong in the world. Some of these include *The Boys, Brightburn, Hancock,* and *Megamind.* These stories share a common theme: Certain individuals possess unparalleled power. Consequently, these individuals often use their superpowers for selfish ambition or to further their own vision, causing abuse and injustice toward those who are less powerful. Ultimately, justice is pursued and, to some extent, realized through a higher power that brings order and necessary restraint. In essence, these fictional stories delve into the realities of abuse that can occur when people relate to one another through power imbalances.

Much like the superhero sagas, we don't have to look far to observe power differentials in our own lives. For example, I quickly learned as a child that my parents, teachers, and other adults had powers, privileges, and responsibilities that I did not share. I had to take naps even when I didn't feel tired. I had to follow instructions simply because I was told to. I had to stand in line at school and avoid causing a commotion in class unless I wanted to face consequences.

It's interesting to reflect on how the early part of my life was about learning to relate to people who had more power than I did. Later, I became aware of my own developing capabilities and powers. A subsequent season involved learning to relate responsibly to peers like my wife, neighbors, and coworkers who shared similar levels of power. Next, I learned to be accountable and relate to those with less power, privilege, and ability than I had.

Through all these life stages, I learned how to relate to authority figures, peers, and subordinates. I came to understand the importance of using my power responsibly, the need for restraint, and the value of a vision bigger than my own ambition. I realized my need for a higher power that offers a perspective demanding meekness and humility, one that orders my actions and all other powers. In short, I learned the dynamics of privilege and power differentials in all my relationships.

How about you?

- Can you see the relational dynamics that play out between you and others who differ in abilities?

The Persecutor's Privilege

- Have you ever missed the mark by using your power to dominate others?

- Have you ever experienced the abuse of power or ability and seen the need for further responsibility, vision, and therefore accountability?

~

Let's explore what our biblical text offers regarding the dynamics of power differentials.

When examining Jonah, we again notice what is not explicitly said about Nineveh. First, we see that few details are provided because the people of Nineveh are not the primary audience or the focus of the book. Instead, the focus is on Jonah's hardened heart and, by extension, Israel, as the audience shares in God's rebuke of Jonah.

Despite this lack of detail about Nineveh and Assyria, we are not left without relevant information to consider. In the subtle margins of Jonah's story, we can reasonably assume a clear power differential between Assyria and other nations, primarily Israel.

These assumptions are confirmed elsewhere in Scripture. For example, in Nahum, often referred to by theologians as "Jonah: The Sequel," Israel is clearly portrayed as less powerful than its enemy, Assyria. The Assyrians operated on a higher level of power, leaving Israel extremely vulnerable to their oppression.

Let us now turn to Nahum 2:5–13, which presents us with God's thoughts on Assyria's use of power over others:

> Nineveh summons her picked troops, yet they stumble on their way. They dash to the city wall; the protective shield is put in place. The river gates are thrown open and the palace collapses. It is decreed that Nineveh be exiled and carried away. Her female slaves moan like doves and beat on their breasts. Nineveh is like a pool whose water is draining away. "Stop! Stop!" they cry, but no one turns back. Plunder the silver! Plunder the gold! The supply is endless, the wealth from all its treasures!

Drowning in Drama

> She is pillaged, plundered, stripped! Hearts melt, knees give way, bodies tremble, every face grows pale.
>
> Where now is the lions' den, the place where they fed their young, where the lion and lioness went, and the cubs, with nothing to fear? The lion killed enough for his cubs and strangled the prey for his mate, filling his lairs with the kill and his dens with the prey.
>
> "I am against you," declares the LORD Almighty. "I will burn up your chariots in smoke, and the sword will devour your young lions. I will leave you no prey on the earth. The voices of your messengers will no longer be heard."

Nahum presents a dynamic of power differentials gone wrong between Assyria and other nations.[1] The author depicts Assyria as a great lion—the king of the animal kingdom—that used its power to prey on others. But we see it here on the brink of its destruction. God is setting things right, declaring that he will no longer tolerate Assyria's predatory use of power, which has been used to enslave and dominate less powerful nations.

Yet in Jonah 3, we see that, at least for a time, Nineveh acknowledges and submits to God's vision for its power. When confronted by God's prophet Jonah, the Ninevites humbly respond and recognize that their power is ultimately subject to God. They surrender their power to align with God's vision, which includes honor, respect, and dignity for others, from the least to the greatest among them.

Let's examine the text again:

> Jonah began by going a day's journey into the city, proclaiming, "Forty more days and Nineveh will be overthrown." The Ninevites believed God. A fast was proclaimed, and all of them, from the greatest to the least, put on sackcloth.
>
> When Jonah's warning reached the king of Nineveh, he rose from his throne, took off his royal robes, covered himself with sackcloth and sat down in the dust. This is the proclamation he issued in Nineveh:

---

1. Cook, "Blessed," 363–68.

The Persecutor's Privilege

> "By the decree of the king and his nobles:
> "Do not let people or animals, herds or flocks, taste anything; do not let them eat or drink. But let people and animals be covered with sackcloth. Let everyone call urgently on God. Let them give up their evil ways and their violence. Who knows? God may yet relent and with compassion turn from his fierce anger so that we will not perish."
>
> When God saw what they did and how they turned from their evil ways, he relented and did not bring on them the destruction he had threatened.

Notice how this chapter highlights the response of all people across different levels of power. For instance, the text states, "all of them, from the greatest to the least." The individuals in Nineveh, each with varying levels of power, freely respond to God with their own agency. While we see the king using his power to command the common people to repent under threat of punishment, we also see the common people responding before the king's edict is even issued. Additionally, the text illustrates some of the levels within the hierarchy of power: the king, nobles, people, and even animals. All these figures, with differing degrees of realized power, are justly ordered by the greater vision of God's call to repentance—a call that benefits not only the greatest but especially the least. This is vividly illustrated in the way the people (great) help the animals (least) to act in accordance with God's will.

This vision is God's invitation for the people of Nineveh to relate rightly with him and to fulfill a purpose greater than their own ambitions. This godly fear of impending destruction righteously orders all other fears, replacing violence with corporate justice and love. By embracing God's vision, the Ninevites no longer equate power with permission. Their repentance trickles down from the greatest to the least, even affecting Israel and other nations of lesser power. For example, Jeroboam II, the king of Israel during Jonah's time, experienced substantial peace and prosperity, as Assyria appears to leave Israel and Judah alone for a considerable period. This peace is presumably a result of Jonah's ministry to Nineveh.

Drowning in Drama

∼

I hope you grasp the idea I am striving to communicate in this chapter. The world comprises individuals and groups who vary in all kinds of power and privilege. The Persecutors in any typical drama possess more power than those they persecute and, therefore, in order to change, must be more aware of those who are vulnerable to their prerogatives. As illustrated in Jonah, those with more power should abandon predatory persecution and instead challenge and support those with less power to fulfill God's vision, as demonstrated when the people of Nineveh help even their animals repent.

It should be noted that Persecutors, like the Ninevites, must remain wholly aware of God's power over them when using their qualified power and limited privileges over others.

In my own life, I found that a vision and healthy fear of God ordered my power and privileges, guiding me to relate properly to those most vulnerable to my prerogatives.

PERSECUTORS AND THEIR POWER DIFFERENTIALS

1. Would you say you have been on the high and/or low ends of power relationships?
2. Do you ever notice the power differentials around you? Where would you place yourself in those relationships?
3. What privileges do you carry into your relationships?

14

A Propensity for Propaganda

How Power Drives the Creation of False Images to Coerce and Control

"People look at the outward appearance, but the LORD looks at the heart."
—1 SAMUEL 16:7

"Every idol, if you scratch it, is a mirror. We worship ourselves."
—(ATTRIBUTED TO) R. C. SPROUL JR.

AS A KID, THE 1939 movie *The Wizard of Oz* amazed me. I remember being both frightened and thrilled by the flying monkeys, the Wicked Witch, and the Wizard. This story, with its adventurous characters, contained many captivating truths. One of those was that the "great and powerful" Wizard of Oz was not as powerful as his projection suggested.

In fact, the Wizard of Oz was an unintentional Persecutor, adding to the drama and fear of others until he was met by Dorothy. This necessary provocation came through the creative vulnerabilities of Dorothy and her friends, which exposed the Wizard's need to surrender his power to a vision larger than his own ambition. His powerful image was merely a projection, an idol, an idea that spread an ideology among others, making them fear Oz and acquiesce to his will. He was, indeed, a Persecutor who used propaganda to fulfill his agenda of self-protection through the coercion of others.

It is only through repeated exposure to Dorothy and her friends—Vulnerable Creators in the Winner's Triangle—that the Wizard abandons his use of propaganda. By doing so, the Wizard exits the Drama Triangle and enters the Winner's Triangle as an Assertive Challenger. He then begins challenging others in a supportive way instead of terrifying or persecuting them. For instance, he assertively encourages the Lion to acknowledge his innate courage, the Tin Man to see that he has the biggest heart of all, and the Scarecrow to recognize the intelligence he never realized he possessed.

In the same way, I have noticed a tendency in Persecutors, like the Wizard of Oz, to cultivate a powerful false image to coerce others. The biggest example in my life is how I have often presented a false self to others—a projection of my own power, competence, and confidence—intended first to protect myself from rejection but ultimately to manipulate others. In short, I have been a Persecutor who used personal propaganda to both protect and coerce.

How about you?

- Have you ever noticed the use of propaganda or public relations by those in power to protect and control?
- Can you relate to presenting a carefully crafted image as a means of projecting power and dominance over others?
- Do you ever find yourself presenting a false self—a social façade that influences others by showcasing the most powerful version of yourself?

∼

A Propensity for Propaganda

Let's consider what Nineveh reveals to us about a Persecutor's use of propaganda. While the literary work of Jonah does not provide much detail regarding Nineveh, we can learn from its artifacts. The Assyrians left numerous reliefs in the walls and gates of Nineveh, which illustrate the historical events, culture, gods, and values of their society. The predominant themes in these reliefs include depictions of violence, power, and warfare. In short, the Assyrians were masters of image-making, idolatry, and propaganda.

The Assyrians documented their powerful and violent exploits through both words and images. They used these displays as powerful propaganda to serve their interests by intimidating others. Examples include pyramids of heads at city gates, enemy skins displayed on walls, limbs nailed to doors, and naked bodies impaled all around—symbols of their power and dominance over those they sought to subdue.

Isaiah 10:5–13 gives us further insight into God's perspective on the Assyrians' use of propaganda, which is driven by their pride.

> "Woe to the Assyrian, the rod of my anger, in whose hand is the club of my wrath! I send him against a godless nation, I dispatch him against a people who anger me, to seize loot and snatch plunder, and to trample them down like mud in the streets. But this is not what he intends, this is not what he has in mind; his purpose is to destroy, to put an end to many nations.
>
> "'Are not my commanders all kings?' he says. 'Has not Kalno fared like Carchemish? Is not Hamath like Arpad, and Samaria like Damascus? As my hand seized the kingdoms of the idols, kingdoms whose images excelled those of Jerusalem and Samaria—shall I not deal with Jerusalem and her images as I dealt with Samaria and her idols?'"
>
> When the Lord has finished all his work against Mount Zion and Jerusalem, he will say, "I will punish the king of Assyria for the willful pride of his heart and the haughty look in his eyes. For he says:
>
> "'By the strength of my hand I have done this, and by my wisdom, because I have understanding. I removed

the boundaries of nations, I plundered their treasures;
like a mighty one I subdued their kings."'

In this text, we notice Assyria's selfish ambition. They claim to have accomplished everything by their own power and solely for their own purposes. They begin to assume the role of God in their lives and in the lives of those less powerful. They present to themselves and others a false self—the idea that their power and desire to act are unqualified (a theological term often used to describe how God is specifically unrestrained and unlimited). However, God clearly takes note of their behavior and diagnoses it as willful pride in the heart and a haughty look in the eyes.

Somewhere between Jonah and Isaiah, Assyria begins to believe its own propaganda, buying into its own spin and press releases. The repentance in Jonah is short-lived. Rather than possessing their power, the Assyrians' power seems to take possession of them. They start focusing on image—the images of others and themselves. They start to idolize their own image, making themselves extremely vulnerable to the inevitable truth that God is an all-powerful God of justice who will indeed judge their prideful abuse of privilege. The self that they believe themselves to be is ultimately false!

A PROBLEM OF PROPAGANDA

1. Have you ever presented a false version of yourself—a façade of power, competence, or confidence—to protect your ego and avoid rejection?
2. Can you recall a time when you used your strengths to subtly manipulate or coerce others to align with your desires? What motivated this behavior?
3. Have you noticed moments in which you prioritized maintaining an image over being more authentic and vulnerable? How did this impact your need for connection?

15

Violent Coercion

Examining the Persecutor's Spectrum of Violence and Urging Self-Reflection

"Do not envy the violent or choose any of their ways."
—Proverbs 3:31

"One who uses coercion is guilty of deliberate violence. Coercion is inhuman."
—Mahatma Gandhi

About fifteen years ago, I had one of my most regrettable failures as a husband and father. That's a sterile way of saying that I abused my power. It was Christmastime, and we were traveling from our home in Connecticut to visit my in-laws for the holiday celebrations. What a Christmas memory this turned out to be—one I hope my family has forgotten among more loving memories.

We had packed into our small SUV and headed south on Interstate 95 for a trip of about five hours to my in-laws'. About an hour away from our destination, my kids decided they were done.

Drowning in Drama

More specifically, my sons began competing, and their conversational rivalry quickly devolved into a verbal bloodbath.

At that moment, I missed the exit I needed to take and found myself feeling completely lost that Christmas Eve. I entered this developing drama initially as a default Rescuer, trying to save my family and each of my sons from the other. But soon, I felt like a Victim, overwhelmed by the situation and, in particular, by one of my boys.

Because I absolutely despise feeling like a Victim, I quickly shifted to the Persecutor role. I reached back while driving, grabbed my son, and tried to intimidate him into submission. This led to some dangerous swerving as I sped down the highway in the night. At that point, my wife turned to me, pleading with me to stop and calm down. But I was flooded with anger, under which lay a fear that my family was falling apart. Now I was lost, not only geographically but also relationally. I had lost control of my emotions and behavior, hurting those I loved most.

I hate to admit it, but it actually took a slap across my cheek from my wife to pull me out of my rage and readiness for violence. That did it. I was at first enraged, but simultaneously challenged! Her slap acted like smelling salts, bringing a much-needed awareness of just how out of control and fearful I had become. I had embraced and even relished the powerful role of the Persecutor.

Not my finest moment. Ultimately, our family found ourselves in a closed McDonald's parking lot, where we slowly transitioned from our roles in the Drama Triangle to those in the Winner's Triangle.

Please tell me you can relate! Maybe not with being physically violent, but perhaps with coercing others through your use of power, manipulation, or even the silent treatment.

How about you?

- Have you ever had a moment of coercive anger in which you became the Persecutor?

Violent Coercion

- Have you ever used either physical or verbal aggression to intimidate or demean others?

∼

Let's explore what the story of Jonah and Nineveh reveals about a Persecutor's tendency toward violent coercion. Interestingly, in my research for this book, every biblical commentator, historian, and theologian I encountered agreed that Assyria (including its capital city of Nineveh) was indeed a cruel and violent empire. It was widely known for its terror and the frequent torture of others.

For instance, the Biblical Archaeological Society noted that Sennacherib, who established Nineveh as the capital of Assyria, may have been one of Assyria's most brutal kings. Here is a self-proclaimed testimony of Sennacherib's violence:

> I cut their throats like lambs. I cut off their precious lives as one cuts a string. Like the many waters of a storm, I made the contents of their gullets and entrails run down upon the wide earth. My prancing steeds harnessed for my riding, plunged into the streams of their blood as into a river. The wheels of my war chariot, which brings low the wicked and the evil, were bespattered with blood and filth. With the bodies of their warriors I filled the plain, like grass. Their testicles I cut off, and tore out their privates like the seeds of cucumbers.[1]

I hesitate to go here, but I feel it's necessary. While reading his shocking descriptions, I can't help but picture what I believe he intends readers to graphically visualize. Sennacherib bluntly compares brutal emasculations to the casual act of harvesting vegetables. More specifically, he likens the removal of male testicles to the imagery of snapping peas or butter beans. This association intentionally triggers in me, and likely in some of you, memories of helping grandmothers and mothers harvest vegetables to prepare a meal—as well as disgust and perhaps even nausea.

---

1. Bleibtreu, "Grisly," 51–62.

Drowning in Drama

I don't believe I'm overreaching here. In fact, I want us to recognize that these brutal images and the feelings they provoke are precisely what Sennacherib intended to evoke as a means of coercion for those who read his words.

Let's consider another violent episode of an ancient Assyrian Persecutor. Erika Bleibtreu explains in her work, "Grisly Assyrian Record of Torture and Death," that Ashurbanipal, a powerful Assyrian king, led some of his captives into slavery by putting fishhooks in their mouths. Moreover, Ashurbanipal often had enemies tied to the ground while their skin was peeled off, and when he tired of their screams, he would silence them by having their tongues cut out.[2]

From these gruesome examples, we can assert that the Assyrians/Ninevites were Persecutors who used violence as a means of achieving their desires.

∼

Let's take a step back from the graphic history of Assyria and look again at the iconic figure of Darth Vader, who archetypically demonstrates the dynamics of violent coercion. Vader is particularly helpful as an example because he represents the spectrum of implicit and explicit violent coercion often used by Persecutors. For instance, he intimidates those closest to him—such as his wife and immediate subordinates—with the "force choke," an implicit use of power that cuts off the air of those he seeks to intimidate, punish, silence, or control. Because the force choke is implicit, meaning he doesn't physically lay a hand on his victims, it can sometimes seem, at least initially, that he isn't doing any harm. Yet even without physical touch, the intended terror and injury to the victim are no less real.

On the other end of the spectrum, Vader also employs explicit (physical) acts of violence and betrayal to assert his power. A prime example is when he uses his leadership and lightsaber

2. Bleibtreu, "Grisly," 51–62.

Violent Coercion

to attack the Jedi Temple, slaughtering all Jedi knights, including younglings.

Like Vader, Persecutors often operate on a spectrum of implicit and explicit violence. This range only heightens the torture, fear, intimidation, and struggle experienced by those who are coerced through persecution.

CONSIDERING OUR COERCION

1. Would those closest to you suggest that you have a tendency for violence?
2. Are you ever afraid enough to consider using violent coercion on others?
3. Do you ever catch yourself violently responding in a rage?

16

Submission of Power

How Surrendering to God's Vision Transforms Personal Power into a Source of True Strength

"Because you have rejected this message, relied on oppression and depended on deceit, this sin will become for you a high wall, cracked and bulging, that collapses suddenly in an instant. It will break to pieces like pottery, shattered mercilessly.... This is what the sovereign LORD, the Holy One, says: 'In repentance and rest is your salvation, in quietness and trust is your strength, but you would have none of it.'"

—ISAIAH 30:12–15

"The greatness of a man's power is the measure of his surrender."

—WILLIAM BOOTH

ONE EVENING SEVERAL YEARS ago, my wife, kids, and friends jokingly brought up my repeated rages. It all began when my kids found a meme of the Incredible Hulk. In the cartoon meme, the Hulk is driving a Jeep, turning toward a commotion in the back seat and yelling in frustration, "You won't like me when I'm angry!"

Submission of Power

Ha ha! I smiled and laughed out loud, thinking of myself, my father, and my grandfathers, who often acted similarly.

At first, their meme-sharing was comical, as they depicted caricatures of my behavior that were relatable to most anyone who has gone on a long road trip with kids. However, as they continued sharing episodes of my outbursts—many of which had occurred in the car—I began to be aware of both my own and their vulnerabilities. I first noticed vulnerability in them; they felt safe enough, using the meme and one another's support, to share their humor, fear, and even hurt about my often unsafe behaviors toward them. Then, I noticed my own pain and sorrow as I came face to face with my failures and their impact on those I loved.

At that moment, I had a choice: I could cultivate a conversation that listened and responded to their comments, or I could do what I had always done—be dismissive and defensive.

By God's grace, I chose to ask genuine questions. As I did, I quickly noticed the grief that made me feel like a Victim. This was my default drama pattern beginning to surface. However, this time, I chose vulnerability and surrendered my power to align with their perspective. I allowed myself to truly hear their views of me, which highlighted the need to realize God's greater vision for my life. This vision—God's hope—was one in which I could become safer for them while remaining assertive when needed. God's vision required only my submission of power to him—or, you could call it, my resting in repentance.

How about you?

- Can you at all relate to your power needing to submit to God's vision?
- Have you ever been challenged by how others receive you and your power?
- Have you ever noticed how your power coerces but doesn't really bring lasting transformation?

Drowning in Drama

Let's look at the text of Jonah once again. Scandalously, the Ninevites' repentance shames Jonah and, in the broader sense, God's own people, the Israelites. The Ninevites provide an example of complete submission to God that should—and does—provoke jealousy and angst in anyone unwilling to respond similarly. In short, the Ninevites exemplify repentance and model what the submission of one's power to God should look like.

Let's take a closer look at Jonah 3:4–10:

> Jonah began by going a day's journey into the city, proclaiming, "Forty more days and Nineveh will be overthrown." The Ninevites believed God. A fast was proclaimed, and all of them, from the greatest to the least, put on sackcloth.
>
> When Jonah's warning reached the king of Nineveh, he rose from his throne, took off his royal robes, covered himself with sackcloth and sat down in the dust. This is the proclamation he issued in Nineveh:
>
> "By the decree of the king and his nobles:
>
> "Do not let people or animals, herds or flocks, taste anything; do not let them eat or drink. But let people and animals be covered with sackcloth. Let everyone call urgently on God. Let them give up their evil ways and their violence. Who knows? God may yet relent and with compassion turn from his fierce anger so that we will not perish."
>
> When God saw what they did and how they turned from their evil ways, he relented and did not bring on them the destruction he had threatened.

From the outset, it's important to recognize that Nineveh's submission to God's vision was sparked by Jonah's actions, even though his effort was reluctant and minimal. Similarly, the submission of Persecutors often begins in response to the vulnerability of a Creator's vision (the Vulnerable Creator being the Victim's foil in the Winner's Triangle). This vulnerability extends an invitation for partnership, calling Persecutors to surrender their power to

Submission of Power

God. Through this surrender, they can discover a greater purpose beyond the confines of their false self.

Although submission is often initiated by a Vulnerable Creator, it is ultimately nurtured and cultivated by the Persecutor. Thus, Nineveh provides us with some characteristics of a Persecutor's response of submission. Let's glean from the elements of Nineveh's submission to God.

First, Nineveh's response is subtractive in nature. For instance, the Ninevites call for a fast in which they determine not to eat or drink. They sit in the dust, waiting on God and hoping he might relent. Additionally, they give up their specific behaviors of violence. In short, they engage in subtractive spiritual disciplines like fasting, silence, resting/waiting, and renouncing certain behaviors.

This subtractive approach is significant because it creates margin, time, and space for them to commune and interact with God. It is a posture of cutting out distractions to listen to God attentively. It's like looking God in the eyes, hoping to grasp all that he might communicate in their vulnerable conversation.

Second, notice that Nineveh's response is characterized by its cultivating a greater sensitivity to God and his word. For example, all the Ninevites put on sackcloth, a coarse material that demonstrates one's willingness to live uncomfortably with pain or grief, hoping it will both motivate and alert them to unknown yet necessary sorrow for deeper transformation. Interestingly, sackcloth combined with subtractive disciplines such as silence, solitude, and waiting work hand in hand to allow one to sit sensitively, fully engrossed in repentance before God.

Settling into this kind of intentional repentance avoids the superficial change that comes when one simply withdraws from discomfort or heightened sensitivity. Thus, avoiding pain, discomfort, and penitence prematurely misses the gift of repentance, which brings thorough and necessary transformation. In other words, resting in penitence ensures that repentance touches not only one's conscious motivations but also one's deeper psyche.

On an important sidenote, I'd argue that this kind of subtractive spiritual discipline is needed in the Western church. Too often,

Drowning in Drama

I've seen leaders, churches, movements, and denominations rush to "handle" their failures through crisis management rather than admit their desire to move on and wait patiently for godly sorrow to alert and motivate more profound transformation.

Experienced repentance remains too often superficial, leaving necessary work unaddressed or unnoticed, which inevitably leads to repeated failures in the future. As Foster describes in *The Celebration of Discipline*, "Only submission can free us sufficiently to enable us to distinguish between genuine issues and stubborn self-will."[1]

Thirdly, we should observe that Nineveh's repentance is characterized by exceptional humility. The king of Nineveh, for instance, humbles himself before God and his people. He puts on sackcloth and sits in the dust, abased before the foreign God of Israel. The Ninevites sit in the dust in the same manner, identifying themselves with their sorrow and helplessness, recognizing that only God can forgive and restore them.

Finally, as mentioned in a previous chapter, the Ninevites' surrender is marked not only by individual repentance but also by the corporate responsibility of the more powerful helping those less powerful to also surrender and repent. This is demonstrated in the king and nobles' decree that all people adopt a similar posture of patient repentance. It is further illustrated by the people aiding their animals in repentance by covering them in sackcloth.

～

Submission is a cultivated response to power. Although surrender is often seen as a fearful response to violence, it's important to remember that surrender can also be an appropriate response to *vision*. When someone vulnerably invites others to join a vision that requires their power, their vulnerability can be reciprocated through the surrender of the others' power to that vision. In this dynamic, power becomes most meaningful and is subsequently

---

1. Foster, *Celebration*, 111.

Submission of Power

scaled up or amplified through partnered strengths focused on a shared ideal. This is when surrender becomes powerful!

In *Return of the Jedi*, Luke and Vader face off in the climax of the *Star Wars* saga. Luke refuses to use his power to dominate Vader. Instead, he makes himself vulnerable to the persecution of the Emperor, which ultimately moves Vader's heart. Vader abandons the dark side and is redeemed by surrendering his power to a greater vision, bringing balance to the Force by overthrowing the Emperor and his dominance.

Likewise, I can personally relate to the need to surrender my power to God's vision through waiting in repentance. This process—called *metanoia* in Greek—requires an openness of the mind and heart to become aware and listen. At one point in my midlife, when the Lord asked me to let him save me from my false ego, I found myself responding, "I want to want to."

In other words, I didn't want to surrender, yet there was a deep part of me that *wanted* to want to. My hope was that God could start there, working with my mixed and layered desires. During that time, I asked him to help me restrain the parts of myself that were still resistant, trusting that he could lead me toward full surrender to his vision.

Perhaps this seems convoluted and difficult to grasp, so let me offer an experience that might clarify what I mean. As I shared earlier, I suffered a fishhook injury to my left eye and underwent multiple surgeries to save my eye and restore my sight. Many people asked me about the pain of the injury itself, but I repeatedly told them that the worst pain came from the process of healing—specifically, the repeated exposure to light as the doctors assessed the damage and performed surgeries.

Time and again, I remember gripping the chair's armrests while my doctor—a highly skilled and compassionate woman—shone bright lights through magnifiers into my injured eye. The pain was excruciating. I often cried, gritting my teeth for what felt like endless minutes, determined not to stand up in a fit of agony and forcibly stop my doctor, who was all of 135 pounds. To this day, that remains the most intense physical pain I've ever endured.

I had to assertively surrender my bodily power to the vision of my doctor, enduring the pain patiently and hoping that my eye could be saved and my sight restored.

∼

Surrendering our power to God's vision paradoxically makes us even more powerful or authoritative, as our strength now draws from a source far greater than our own. In fact, it is rooted in the ultimate source—God and his boundless love for others.

I experienced this truth vividly during a church split in my first pastorate. At the time, I felt as though I was in a battle, not only fighting for myself but also for others who I believed were being genuinely mistreated in the conflict. It was during this season of turmoil that I came across a timely passage in Joshua 5.

In the story, Joshua stands on the far side of the Jordan River, preparing for what he believes will be a battle against the people of Jericho. At that critical moment, an angel of the Lord appears to him. Naturally, Joshua asks, "Are you for us or against us?" But in a manner characteristic of God's wisdom, the angel essentially responds, "You're looking at this the wrong way. This is not your battle, but mine." The question is, whose side are you on? The angel's message reframes the situation entirely. Instead of focusing on whether God is on our side, we are called to align ourselves with what God is already doing and trust him to lead the fight.

This perspective was transformative for me. It reminded me that true power comes not from striving in our own strength but from surrendering to God's purposes and standing behind his leadership. This posture exemplifies the role of the Assertive Challenger in the Winner's Triangle—one who acts with courage and conviction, not from personal ambition, but from a deep alignment with God's will and a trust in his ultimate authority.[2]

∼

---

2. Choy, "Winner's Triangle," 45.

Submission of Power

Let's look at the story of Jonah all over again, but this time as told by Jesus. We'll see how the Ninevites, once Persecutors, become Assertive Challengers submitted to God's vision in Matthew 12:38–41 (emphasis added):

> Then some of the Pharisees and teachers of the law said to him, "Teacher, we want to see a sign from you."
> He answered, "A wicked and adulterous generation asks for a sign! But none will be given it except the sign of the prophet Jonah. For as Jonah was three days and three nights in the belly of a huge fish, so the Son of Man will be three days and three nights in the heart of the earth. *The men of Nineveh will stand up at the judgment with this generation and condemn it; for they repented at the preaching of Jonah, and now something greater than Jonah is here.*"

The Ninevites' story in the book of Jonah and Jesus's reference to it invite us to consider how we might submit our power to God's vision in our own lives. True submission to God is not passive or weak; it requires first the courage to confront our sin, to let go of our stubborn self-will, and to embrace the transformative power of God's grace. It also calls us to recognize in our relationships the assertive role we can take that does not seek to dominate or coerce but to heal and restore through love and sacrifice.

By embracing this kind of submission, we can, like the Ninevites, become Assertive Challengers for God's vision in our world, standing as a testament to his redemptive power and challenging others to see the greatness of his kingdom. In doing so, we honor Jesus, the "something [someone] greater than Jonah" who came to bring salvation to all.

SURRENDERING POWER

1. When have you masked pain or fear with control or intensity, and what would it look like to pause and listen instead?

Drowning in Drama

2. Where might God be inviting you to practice "subtractive" disciplines like silence, waiting, or repentance in order to create space for his vision to take root?

3. Have you ever been afraid to submit your power—even to God—because you didn't fully want to surrender? Can you, at the very least, begin with "I want to want to"?

4. How can you move from reacting as a Victim, Rescuer, or Persecutor to responding as an Assertive Challenger, surrendered to God's vision and aligned with his redemptive love?

Part 4

Christ and the Winner's Triangle

17

Our Vulnerable Creator

*Revealing Jesus as the One Who
Breaks the Cycle of Drama*

"[Now] something greater than Jonah is here[!]"
—LUKE 11:32

"God has a heart. He can feel, and be affected. He is not impassable. He cannot be moved from outside by an extraneous power. But this does not mean that He is not capable of moving Himself. No, God is moved and stirred, yet not like ourselves in powerlessness, but in His own free power...."
—KARL BARTH, *CHURCH DOGMATICS*

IN THIS FOURTH PART and final chapter of the book, I migrate from one biblical sense of interpretation to another. Instead of looking at the book of Jonah through a tropological sense, I utilize a Christological sense. A Christological sense interprets Scripture through the primary lens of Christ and the work of the triune God in the incarnation, death, and resurrection of Jesus.

Drowning in Drama

While the first three parts of this book unpack the Drama Triangle through the narrative of Jonah, this fourth and final part considers the Winner's Triangle as demonstrated in the narratives of Christ. I will both compare and contrast Jonah's default roles in the Drama Triangle with Jesus's roles in the Winner's Triangle.

Whereas Jonah entered his drama as a Victim, transitioned to Persecutor, and only reluctantly cared to coach, Jesus entered as a Vulnerable Creator who caringly coaches and assertively challenges when needed. In short, while Jonah was an actor in the Drama Triangle, Christ embodies the Winner's Triangle.

Or, better said, Christ resolves the world's drama.

Christ succeeded where Jonah fell short; he demonstrated a perfected path beyond life's relational dramas. In light of this, I would suggest that Jonah's story serves as both an antitype and archetype of Christ, offering us a model of surrender, vulnerability, and reliance on God's power, ultimately pointing us toward a life that mirrors Christ's peace and fulfills his purpose for us all.

~

At the beginning of this book, I shared how my wife's courageous choice to respond with vulnerability became a blueprint for the "winner's life"—one free from the entanglements of the Drama Triangle. Her example, combined with the story of Jonah and insights from various relational theories, gave me a powerful vision of what life and relationships could look like. At the heart of my revelation was a deep invitation from Christ himself. Jesus was vulnerably opening new paths for me to a free and vibrant life. He was inviting me to surrender my hurt, my control, and my power to him.

My hope is that you may have also sensed a similar invitation while reading this book. May the Vulnerable Creator, Christ himself, be engaging in your dramas, inviting you into new patterns of relating to him and others.

How about you?

- Is the Vulnerable Creator inviting you to exit the Drama Triangle and follow him into the Winner's Triangle?
- How have you begun to notice Christ's default Winner's Triangle pattern—how he enters our human drama as the Vulnerable Creator?

∼

Let's take a look at Matthew 12:38–43, and see how Christ relates to and succeeds Jonah as a Vulnerable Creator:

> Then some of the Pharisees and teachers of the law said to him, "Teacher, we want to see a sign from you."
> He answered, "A wicked and adulterous generation asks for a sign! But none will be given it except the sign of the prophet Jonah. For as Jonah was three days and three nights in the belly of a huge fish, so the Son of Man will be three days and three nights in the heart of the earth. The men of Nineveh will stand up at the judgment with this generation and condemn it; for they repented at the preaching of Jonah, and now something greater than Jonah is here. The Queen of the South will rise at the judgment with this generation and condemn it; for she came from the ends of the earth to listen to Solomon's wisdom, and now something greater than Solomon is here.
> "When an impure spirit comes out of a person, it goes through arid places seeking rest and does not find it. Then it says, 'I will return to the house I left.' When it arrives, it finds the house unoccupied, swept clean and put in order. Then it goes and takes with it seven other spirits more wicked than itself, and they go in and live there. And the final condition of that person is worse than the first. That is how it will be with this wicked generation."

In this passage, we find Jesus relating to Jonah as someone who is sent to preach repentance. Jesus, like Jonah, is mercifully sent by the Father to save not only Jews but also the enemies of God: the Gentiles. Jesus, again like Jonah, receives a death sentence

Drowning in Drama

and a resurrection that acts as a powerful sign to those to whom he is sent. Like Jonah, Jesus experiences real hurt and is asked by God to surrender that hurt to the Father's purposes.

However, unlike Jonah, Jesus succeeds in becoming a Vulnerable Creator. He surrenders his life in trust of God's character and vulnerably faces his pain, creating for all of us—through his death, burial, and resurrection—a new way of relating.

Jesus was arguably the most victimized person in history. In fact, Christianity holds to the assumption that he experienced the greatest human drama. Yet the larger gospel narrative shows us that God, in his profound love and vulnerability, chose to enter this drama by becoming flesh, fully embracing our human experience in solidarity, suffering as the ultimate Victim.

Unlike humanity, God did not choose to perpetuate this Adamic drama that began in the Garden of Eden. Instead, through Jesus, he chose the path of the Winner's Triangle. Through his vulnerability on the cross, the triune God opened a way for all of creation to escape the cycle of drama and step into the freedom of a winner's life.

This is the crux of the gospel, as several theologians note. For example, Hans Urs von Balthasar's *Theo-Drama* defines the events of Christ's life as a cosmic drama in which God takes on human sin, suffering, and death in an act of redemptive love. Balthasar describes the cross as an "emptying" of divine power and a reorientation of drama itself. In this divine drama, Jesus models a way out of conflict and self-centeredness. Instead of playing into the roles of Victim, Persecutor, and Rescuer, Jesus embodies what Balthasar calls a "dramatic transcendence"—God's radical entry into human suffering to bring freedom.[1]

Likewise, Karl Barth emphasizes the "humanity of God" in Jesus Christ, showing God's profound identification with human suffering and vulnerability. He contends that in the incarnation and crucifixion, God chooses to meet humanity where it is most broken and powerless. According to Barth, Christ's willingness to

---

1. See *Theo-Drama: Theological Dramatic Theory* by Hans Urs von Balthasar.

Our Vulnerable Creator

embrace humanity's drama does not end in despair but in God's ultimate victory over sin and death, offering a path for humanity to transcend victimhood. In short, Jesus, in his suffering, does not perpetuate the cycle of drama but rather reveals God's desire for reconciliation and transformation.[2]

Additionally, Jürgen Moltmann's *The Crucified God* frames Jesus as the God who suffers with humanity, entering fully into human drama as the ultimate act of solidarity. According to Moltmann, Jesus's crucifixion demonstrates that God is not distant but fully present in human suffering. By embracing the cross, Jesus broke the cycle of retribution and opened a path for humans to transcend victimhood by entrusting their pain to God, who has already borne it. Moltmann's emphasis on God's identification with Victims suggests that Jesus's choice to endure suffering and rejection without resorting to control or coercion is the ultimate model for exiting the Drama Triangle and entering a life of redemptive harmony with others.[3]

~

In this Winner's Triangle, Jesus provides a model for each of us. Through his vulnerability, Christ becomes the Creator who lights the way out of drama and into a life of true peace and purpose.

This act of surrender not only fulfills God's redemptive plan but also serves as a powerful sign, foreshadowed in the story of Jonah. Like Jonah's journey, Jesus's invitation speaks to those humble enough to listen, while it also assertively rebukes the hardened and prideful. It could be held that Christ's default pattern is, in fact, the Winner's Triangle by which he enters the world drama first as the Vulnerable Creator—the embodied Truth, the incarnated God—and transitions simultaneously to the humble as a Caring Coach and to the prideful as an Assertive Challenger.

---

2. See *The Humanity of God* by Karl Barth.

3. See *The Crucified God: The Cross of Christ as the Foundation and Criticism of Christian Theology* by Jürgen Moltmann.

Drowning in Drama

Through his own vulnerable sacrifice, Jesus completes what Jonah's story could only hint at. He beckons us to lay down our defenses and assume a posture of openness and humility. In this space of surrender, we find more than an escape from judgment: we enter a transformative embrace of God's mercy. Jonah's journey thus foreshadows the radical invitation Christ offers: a path that breaks the cycle of drama and draws each heart into the vulnerability, surrender, and renewal that can only be found in him.

Bibliography

Barth, Karl. *The Humanity of God.* Translated by John Newton Thomas and Thomas Wieser. Louisville, KY: Westminster John Knox, 1960.
Beattie, Melody. *Codependent No More: How to Stop Controlling Others and Start Caring for Yourself.* Center City, MN: Hazelden, 1986.
Bleibtreu, Erika. "Grisly Assyrian Record of Torture and Death." *Biblical Archaeology Review* 17 no. 1 (1991) 52–61.
Bloesch, Donald G. *Freedom for Obedience: Evangelical Ethics in Contemporary Times.* San Francisco, CA: Harper & Row, 1987.
Bonhoeffer, Dietrich. *Life Together: The Classic Exploration of Christian Community.* Translated by John W. Doberstein. San Francisco, CA: Harper & Row, 1954.
Brito, Uri, and Rich Lusk. *The Reluctant Prophet: Jonah Through New Eyes.* Through New Eyes Bible Commentaries. West Monroe, LA: Athanasius, 2021.
Brown, Brené. *Braving the Wilderness: The Quest for True Belonging and the Courage to Stand Alone.* New York: Random House, 2017.
———. "The Power of Vulnerability." TED Talk, Houston, TX, June 2010. 20 min., 2 sec. https://www.ted.com/talks/brene_brown_the_power_of_vulnerability?subtitle=en.
———. *The Gifts of Imperfection.* New York: Random House, 2020.
Camus, Albert. *The Plague.* Translated by S. Gilbert. London: Hamish Hamilton, 1948.
Chambers, Oswald. *My Utmost for His Highest.* New York: Dodd, Mead, & Co., 1935.
Choy, A. "The Winner's Triangle." *Transactional Analysis Journal*, 20, no. 1 (1990) 40–46. https://doi.org/10.1177/036215379002000105.
Clinton, Tim, and Gary Sibcy. *Attachments: Why You Love, Feel, and Act the Way You Do.* Brentwood, TN: Thomas Nelson, 2002.
Cook, Gregory D. "Blessed Be Assyria: Implications of Nahum's Allusion to Babel." *Answers Research Journal* 9 (2016) 363–68.

Bibliography

Edwards, Gareth, dir. *Rogue One: A Star Wars Story*. Lucasfilm, 2016.
Foster, Richard J. *Celebration of Discipline: The Path to Spiritual Growth*. New York: Harper & Row, 1988.
Frahm, Eckart. *Assyria: The Rise and Fall of the World's First Empire*. 4th ed. New York: Basic, 2023.
Grayson, Kirk A. "Assyria and Babylonia." *Orientalia nova series* 49, no. 2 (1980) 140–94.
Hauerwas, Stanley. *Vision and Virtue: Essays in Christian Ethical Reflection*. Notre Dame, IN: University of Notre Dame, 1981.
Hom, Mary Katherine Y. H. "'. . . a Mighty Hunter Before YHWH': Genesis 10:9 and the Moral-Theological Evaluation of Nimrod." *Vetus Testamentum* 60, no. 1 (2010) 63–68. https://doi.org/10.1163/004249310X12577537066918.
Howard, Byron, and Jared Bush, dirs. *Encanto*. Walt Disney Animation Studios, 2021.
Karpman, Stephen B. "Fairy Tales and Script Drama Analysis." *Transactional Analysis Bulletin* 7, no. 26 (1968) 39–43.
Knight, Kevin. *The Summa Theologiae of St. Thomas Aquinas*. Translated by Fathers of the English Dominican Province. New Advent, 2017. https://www.newadvent.org/summa/.
Lembke, Anna. *Dopamine Nation: Finding Balance in the Age of Indulgence*. New York: Dutton, 2021.
Lowry, Lois. *The Giver*. Boston: Houghton Mifflin Harcourt, 1993.
Lucas, George. *Star Wars: Episode 3—Revenge of the Sith*. 20th Century Fox, 2005.
Luibheid, Colm. *Pseudo-Dionysius: The Works of Dionysius the Areopagite*. Mahway, NJ: Paulist, 1987.
Moltmann, Jürgen. *The Crucified God: The Cross of Christ as the Foundation and Criticism of Christian Theology*. Minneapolis, MN: Fortress, 1993.
Moore, Thomas. *Care of the Soul: A Guide for Cultivating Depth and Sacredness in Everyday Life*. New York: Harper Perennial, 2016.
Nouwen, Henri J. M. *The Inner Voice of Love: A Journey Through Anguish to Freedom*. New York: Image, 1996.
Prochaska, J. O., and C. C. DiClemente. "The Transtheoretical Model of Health Behavior Change: Progress and Prospects." *American Journal of Health Promotion* 12, no. 1 (1997) 38–48.
Rotter, Julian B. "Generalized Expectancies for Internal Versus External Control of Reinforcement." *Psychological Monographs: General and Applied* 80, no. 1 (1966) 1–28. https://doi.org/10.1037/h0092976.
Stanton, Andrew, dir. *Finding Nemo*. Pixar Animation Studios, 2003.
Thompson, Curt. *Anatomy of the Soul: Surprising Connections Between Neuroscience and Spiritual Practices That Can Transform Your Life and Relationships*. Carol Stream, IL: SaltRiver, 2010.
van der Kooij, Arie. "The City of Babel and Assyrian Imperialism Genesis 11: 1–9 Interpreted in the Light of Mesopotamian Sources." *Congress Volume Leiden 2004*. Leiden, The Netherlands: Brill, 2006. https://doi.org/10.1163/9789047408772_002.

Bibliography

von Balthasar, Hans Urs. *Theo-Drama: Theological Dramatic Theory.* Vol. 4. San Francisco, CA: Ignatius, 1994.

Weiss, Robert. *Prodependence: Moving Beyond Codependency.* Deerfield Beach, FL: Health Communications, 2018.

Willard, Dallas. *The Spirit of the Disciplines: Understanding How God Changes Lives.* San Francisco, CA: HarperOne, 1991.

www.ingramcontent.com/pod-product-compliance
Lightning Source LLC
Chambersburg PA
CBHW072152160426
43197CB00012B/2351